Readers Theatre for African American History

Recent titles in Teacher Ideas Press
Readers Theatre Series

Just Deal with It! Funny Readers Theatre for Life's Not-So-Funny Moments
Diana R. Jenkins

How and Why Stories for Readers Theatre
Judy Wolfman

Born Storytellers: Readers Theatre Celebrates the Lives and Literature of Classic Authors
Ann N. Black

Around the World Through Holidays: Cross Curricular Readers Theatre
Written and Illustrated by Carol Peterson

Wings of Fancy: Using Readers Theatre to Study Fantasy Genre
Joan Garner

Nonfiction Readers Theatre for Beginning Readers
Anthony D. Fredericks

Mother Goose Readers Theatre for Beginning Readers
Anthony D. Fredericks

MORE Frantic Frogs and Other Frankly Fractured Folktales for Readers Theatre
Anthony D. Fredericks

Songs and Rhymes Readers Theatre for Beginning Readers
Anthony D. Fredericks

Readers Theatre for Middle School Boys: Investigating the Strange and Mysterious
Ann N. Black

African Legends, Myths, and Folktales for Readers Theatre
Anthony D. Fredericks

Against All Odds: Readers Theatre for Grades 3-8
Suzanne I. Barchers and Michael Ruscoe

Readers Theatre for African American History

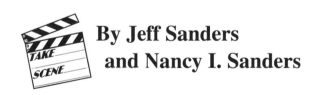 By Jeff Sanders
and Nancy I. Sanders

Readers Theatre

Teacher Ideas Press

An imprint of Libraries Unlimited
Westport, Connecticut • London

Library of Congress Cataloging-in-Publication Data

Sanders, Jeff.
   Readers theatre for African American history / by Jeff Sanders and Nancy I. Sanders.
      p. cm. — (Readers theatre)
    Includes bibliographical references.
    ISBN 978-1-59158-693-7 (alk. paper)
    1. African Americans—History—Study and teaching. 2. African Americans—Biography—Study and teaching. 3. African Americans—History—Juvenile drama. 4. African Americans—Biography—Juvenile drama. 5. Readers' theater. 6. Young adult drama, American. I. Sanders, Nancy I. II. Title.
    E184.7.S26   2008
    973'.0496073'0071—dc22   2008006045

British Library Cataloguing in Publication Data is available.

Library of Congress Catalog Card Number: 2008006045
ISBN: 978-1-59158-693-7

First published in 2008

Libraries Unlimited/Teacher Ideas Press, 88 Post Road West, Westport, CT 06881
A Member of the Greenwood Publishing Group, Inc.
www.teacherideaspress.com
www.lu.com

Printed in the United States of America

∞™

The paper used in this book complies with the
Permanent Paper Standard issued by the National
Information Standards Organization (Z39.48–1984).

10 9 8 7 6 5 4 3 2 1

Contents

Preface vii

Introduction ix

Africa's Glories
Abubakari and the Empire of Mali 1

The American Revolution
Heroes and Patriots 7

Founding Fathers
Richard Allen and the Free African Society 13

Abolitionists
Robert and Harriet (Forten) Purvis Help Lead the Fight 19

The Black Press
The North Star Shines a Bright Light 27

Settling the West
Bass Reeves Keeps the Law 35

Civil War
Emancipation Day on the South Carolina Sea Islands 43

Politics
United States Senators 49

Tuskegee Airmen
True American Heroes 57

The Great Migration
Moving North to a Better Life 63

Harlem Renaissance
Zora Neale Hurston and the Rent Party 71

The Great Debate
Booker T. Washington and W.E.B. Du Bois Lead the Way 79

Holidays
Juneteenth: A Historic Day 87

Science and Medicine
A Scientist Hall of Fame. 95

Inventors
Lewis Latimer Helps Give Light to the World 101

Sports
Jackie Robinson Integrates Baseball 109

Literature
Phillis Wheatley and Famous Poets of Yesterday 117

Visual Arts
Augusta Savage Shapes Her World   125

Music
Marian Anderson's Voice Rings Out 131

The Civil Rights Movement
The March on Washington 137

Teacher Resources. 143
Selected Bibliography 145

Preface

As a public school teacher for more than 25 years, Jeff Sanders knows the importance of making history come alive for his students. Boys and girls in his classroom experience thrill and excitement and also have an opportunity for heightened practical learning when the classroom is transformed into different historic communities throughout the year. Buildings are painted on butcher paper and hung from the ceiling. Authentic recipes are cooked by parent volunteers and brought in to share. Basic costumes are crafted and worn. Students might work at a store to sell goods, at a restaurant to serve food, or dress up as historical characters to offer an eventful surprise—depending on which unit of American history they are currently studying.

Nancy I. Sanders is an award-winning author who specializes in writing about African American history for kids. Her book, *A Kid's Guide to African American History: With over 70 Activities* (Chicago Review Press, 2nd ed., 2007) is bursting with historically based activities that encourage children to experience what life was really like for African Americans who lived during key events in the history of our nation.

Together as a teacher and author, husband and wife team, Jeff and Nancy are dedicated to presenting social studies education as a hands-on and interactive learning environment within the classroom. African American history, especially, is rich with opportunity for students to explore and learn about in a creative learning process. University academia and research is exploding with findings about little-known or nearly forgotten achievements and accomplishments by African Americans. The intermediate level classroom (Grades 4–8) is the perfect setting to introduce these findings to future leaders of our nation. And what better method to actively engage growing minds with new information than to present it in a relevant and interactive approach?

With this book, students can become involved in learning about African American history in a meaningful way. *Readers Theatre for African American History* features a collection of twenty scripts for readers theatre covering a comprehensive span of history from Africa before the trans-Atlantic slave trade on up to include current events in our nation. By participating in these scripts, students will listen to griots—storytellers from Africa—share the rich oral tradition about wealthy explorers who came to the Americas from Africa *before* Columbus. They'll experience Emancipation Day on the South Carolina Sea Islands where Charlotte Forten gathered with others to celebrate the glorious event. They'll attend an imaginary political convention where they'll meet our nation's first five African American U.S. Senators, including Senator Barack Obama.

The scripts contained in this book offer you the opportunity to stimulate your students to learn actively about important people and events in African American history that affect every citizen of our nation in a powerful way. Following each script is a list of possible extension activities to further enhance the learning process. Readers theatre scripts provide the natural ingredient to help bring history alive in your very own classroom.

—Jeff and Nancy I. Sanders

Introduction

Readers Theatre: The Dynamic Duo

Teachers everywhere are discovering the dynamic duo for building reading fluency—combining reading and drama within the classroom environment. The medium is readers theatre, and the outcome produces stronger reading skills and enthusiastic participation from even the most reluctant reader. Easily adaptable to work across the curriculum, readers theatre also helps utilize literature-based learning while studying other subjects such as history, science, and social studies.

If you haven't yet incorporated readers theatre into your intermediate level classroom, you'll soon discover how easy—and rewarding—using readers theatre can be. Follow the tips and suggestions in this section to help you make the most of this book while minimizing the time and preparation it takes to assimilate this valuable learning tool into your lesson plans.

If you're one of the many teachers who already knows and enjoys the benefits of utilizing readers theatre scripts as part of the learning process, this section contains nuggets of gold to help your classroom experience become even better. You'll find tips, strategies, and suggestions to help you conduct successful readers theatre performances with students at varying levels of reading fluency. The goal is to provide you with the inspiration and practical tools you'll need to take your students on a literature-based journey to gain confidence and build important reading skills to help them progress to newfound levels of achievement and self-worth.

Preparing the Script

Duplicate enough copies of the script for each student or pairs of students to have during practice sessions, plus a few extra sets. During the actual performance, however, the audience does not need to hold a script. This helps them better observe and enjoy the actual performance. If you are limited in the amount of copies you can make, consider teaming up with another teacher and share scripts between classrooms.

Introducing the Script

As you introduce a new readers theatre script to your students, follow these steps to help students prepare to practice reading the script aloud:

- Distribute copies of the script and instruct students to read silently through it.

- Make a vocabulary list of the script's unfamiliar or difficult words. Have students look up the definitions, and invite volunteers to read the definitions aloud and discuss the meaning of each word.

• Rehearse important drama techniques with students that will help readers theatre come alive for the characters who are performing as well as for the audience. Select one line of dialogue from the script. Ask volunteers to read the same line aloud with a different emotion or expression in their tone of voice such as anger, worry, fear, happiness, sorrow, excitement, boredom, shyness, weakness, or in a mean and forceful way. Discuss and demonstrate different facial expressions. Choose another line from the script and ask volunteers to read the same line aloud with different facial expressions that show different emotions. Finally, explain that body language also is a powerful tool to use during readers theatre to convey emotion. Lifting your chin, turning your back to someone, pointing, or slouching are just some of the ways body language can be used during the performance. Select another line from the script and ask volunteers to read the same line aloud using varying forms of body language to express different emotions.

Practicing the Script

Some teachers find that a school-week schedule provides the perfect framework for readers theatre. On Monday, the script is introduced to the students. Tuesday through Thursday can be used as practice days. On Friday, students perform the script.

There are different ways for students to practice reading the script. Repeated opportunities for practice help students gain confidence as readers and build important reading skills as they work toward the goal of reading fluency. Whether practicing together as a class or dividing up into small groups, each repeated reading and practice session has its own benefits.

Shared reading can take many forms. With the teacher leading, each student follows along with his or her own script. You can pause to explain vocabulary words, historic meaning, or unfamiliar terms. Depending on the age and reading level of your students, you can incorporate choral reading by alternating back and forth between parts you read and parts being read in unison by the entire class. You can assign groups of students to read various parts in unison. A round-robin approach can give each student in turn the opportunity to read aloud.

After students are familiar with the script, you can choose either to work on it together as a class or divide up into small groups. Each small group may practice the same script or work on different ones that you have introduced.

To assign parts to different students, hold tryouts, ask for volunteers, or simply assign each role. Allow time for students to practice reading their parts in preparation for the performance. Many students may benefit from underlining or highlighting their own parts. As they practice and participate in repeated readings, some students may inadvertently memorize their parts. Because the goal of readers theatre is to practice and develop reading skills, however, don't encourage memorization. Emphasize that characters in readers theatre should always follow along with the script and read their parts aloud. This helps build reading fluency.

Some students may enjoy participating in the role of director during these practice sessions. Volunteer directors can be assigned the part of the narrator to stay in the reading loop. Student directors can listen to tryouts and assign parts. Directors can lead discussions about which tone of voice, facial expressions, and body language might work best for different parts of the script. They can oversee staging, position of characters, and switching of props or simple settings between scenes. Especially with older or more advanced students, incorporating directors into the readers theatre classroom experience can offer an exciting challenge.

Performing the Script

If you choose to use costumes or props, you can use as simple or as elaborate ones as you decide. Here are ideas for simple accessories to add interest to the scripts:

Costumes

Readers theatre in its simplest form requires no costumes. Keeping costumes at a minimum helps maintain the focus on building better reading skills. However, some teachers and students do enjoy adding simple costumes such as:

- Men's suit vests make it easier for the audience to identify male characters, especially if they are performed by girls.

- Scarves, gloves, hats, aprons, and costume jewelry are simple to store yet effective to wear.

- Nametags can help students in the audience better identify the characters during the performance. Write the name of the character with permanent marker on strips of wide masking tape to wear as a nametag, or use purchased nametag stickers from an office supply store. You may also purchase a classroom set of plastic nametag badges and reuse the badges by having students design their own paper inserts for each new performance. A sturdy paper nametag worn as a necklace with a string of yarn also works.

Props

No props are required for a successful readers theatre, but if you choose to add simple ones, donations or thrift store finds can provide used telephones, mikes from karaoke machines for announcers to pretend to use, or other items.

On with the Show!

Readers theatre scripts can be performed in as simple or as elaborate a way as you want. All students in the script may stand or sit on stools in a row in front of the audience. The character or characters who are currently speaking can face the audience while the others stand or sit with their backs to the audience. When it is their turn to speak, they can turn to face the audience as well. When finished, they can turn away.

Simple staging suggestions are provided in this book for each of the scripts if you choose to create a more formal arrangement of the characters as they interact on stage. Music stands provide a place for students to put their scripts as they read. A podium, stand, or desk is especially useful for the narrator who stays in one place on the staging area during the performance. Construction paper folders to hold the scripts lend an air of professionalism. Instruct performers to hold their folders low enough so the audience can see their face to watch their eyes and better hear their voice. Practice entering and exiting the staging area if the script calls for it.

To help the audience connect with the characters and understand the performance better, it might help to begin performances by introducing each student and the character's name he or she will be portraying.

Encourage students to read their parts with as much dramatic expression and enthusiasm as possible.

Evaluating the Script

After the performance, a classroom discussion to evaluate the script is helpful for students to gain a better understanding. Discuss any questions about events or situations portrayed within the script. Compliment performers on jobs well done. Talk about strengths and weaknesses of the elements of the performance including the actual script, expressive reading, props or costumes, and staging.

For added interest, organize a "Readers Theatre Review." Students can post comments on the review to share what they liked about the performance as well as offer concrete and helpful suggestions for improvement. These reviews can be posted on a class Web site or printed out as a newsletter.

If you prefer to have a more formal evaluation of each performance, distribute evaluation forms for students to fill out. Be sure to include the title and author's name of the script and the names of each character at the top of the page. Have students evaluate the introduction, expressive reading, staging, props or costumes, and overall presentation.

Want to Do More?

To encourage students to enjoy readers theatre on their own, prepare several special backpacks to keep in the classroom. Fill each backpack with enough copies for students to perform a script together. Add simple props or costume accessories in the pockets of the backpack. Store backpacks in a center or a corner of the room that has been set up as a mini-stage with stools and music stands. Invite a small group of students who finish classroom work early to visit the center. Have them choose one backpack and practice performing the script it contains. Periodically change the contents of the backpacks to contain new scripts and accessories.

Script Binders

Provide binders for students to collect the various scripts they have performed. Over the year, encourage small groups to switch parts and perform the script again. At the end of the year, host a "Readers Theatre Extravaganza." Invite students to perform their favorite scripts for an audience of another class or invited guests.

Impromptu Performances

Readers theatre is a great activity to incorporate into your schedule to fill in a few extra minutes. Simply keep copies of scripts on hand. When your schedule permits, distribute scripts to students and assign parts. Students may read their parts aloud from their seats or stand at the front of the room. When finished, switch parts if time permits and read the script again.

Create Your Own

One of the exciting challenges of readers theatre is to create your own scripts. At first, students may feel more comfortable writing scripts based on familiar stories such as fairy tales or folktales. As they gain experience, they can start to create their own original scripts.

If you choose to use selections of published children's literature to create your own scripts, look for portions containing unique characters and interesting dialog. To avoid confusion, omit unnecessary parts such as dialogue tags such as "he said" or "she said." Assign the narrative portions of the text to the narrator.

Nonfiction books can be used as readers theatre scripts, too. Simply divide text into small parts and assign different portions of text to different readers. Even the most straightforward expository text can benefit from the creative and dramatic reading a script provides.

Africa's Glories

Abubakari and the Empire of Mali

Staging

Seat the three griots (GREE-awts) on stools in the center of the stage. The children can be seated on the floor in front of them, facing the griots with their backs to the audience. The narrator can be standing at a podium, desk, or music stand on the right of the stage.

Characters

Narrator   Griots 1, 2, and 3
Children

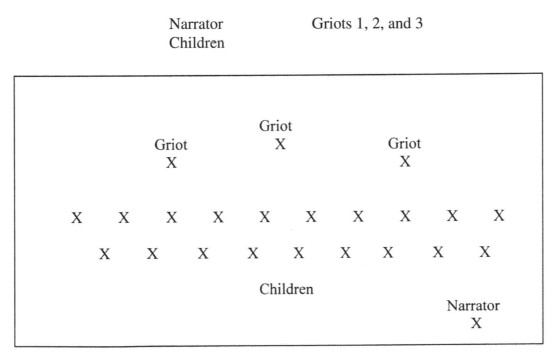

Narrator: During the Middle Ages, kingdoms rose and fell all over the known world. The Plague killed people by the thousands. Marco Polo became famous for his travels to the Far East. In Africa, the home of crocodiles, giraffes, and elephants, great and powerful empires ruled the land. Come and hear griots, or storytellers, from Africa tell about the wonders of Africa's glories in this fictitious scene.

Griot 1: Come everyone! Gather around us today.
Come hear our stories. We have much to say.

Griot 2: Our fathers' words, we believe are true.
We want to tell their words to you.

Griot 3: Our history is a glorious one!
Of scholars, riches, and battles won.

Children: Tell us what happened so long ago.
Tell us, wise ones, for we want to know.

Griot 1: Long, long ago, three great kingdoms ruled the land south of the great desert in Africa. The kingdoms were famous throughout the known world for their great wealth, riches, and gold.

Griot 2: First the kingdom of Ghana ruled from around the ninth to thirteenth centuries. Then the kingdom of Mali ruled during the thirteenth and fourteenth centuries. And finally, the Songhay kingdom rose to power and ruled during the fifteenth and sixteenth centuries.

Griot 3: Great kings reigned over these glorious empires. Our fathers told us of one king, the famous king of Mali. His name was Abubakari the Second. He ruled over a vast land rich with copper mines and gold.

Children: Tell us your story, for we want to hear.
Tell us everything that happened there.

Griot 1: Caravans of more than 10,000 camels traveled from the North. Across the dry, hot Sahara desert they came, blowing in to Abubakari's empire like ships sailing across a sea of sand.

Griot 2: The camels carried heavy loads of wondrous goods on their backs. They brought fabric, grains, and fruits. They brought salt, worth its weight in gold.

Griot 3: Gold is what they wanted. Gold and copper and precious metals. Nowhere else in all the world could the traders find as many riches as they found in the kingdom of Mali.

Children: Tell us more about this glorious land.
Tell us more so we can understand.

Griot 1: The empire of Mali also had great cities that were centers of learning. One of these cities was Timbuktu. It was famous for its libraries. It was famous for its schools. Scholars traveled to Timbuktu from far and wide to study and learn.

Griot 2: Abubakari, the great king of Mali, was a scholar. He had no interest in armies or battles or conquests of gold. He was interested in learning. He was interested in news from the scholars at Timbuktu.

Griot 3: A fantastic story came from Timbuktu to tickle the ears of Abubakari. The story said the earth was round like a gourd. The story said that if someone sailed west across the vast waters of the great Atlantic sea, they would one day reach land.

Children: Tell us what happened to this great, rich king.
Tell us the news. Tell us everything!

Griot 1: So it was that Abubakari turned his eyes to the west. He decided to sail across the great waters and follow the path of the setting sun.

Griot 2: Preparations for an amazing journey took place. Ships were designed and built. Scholars and men of the sea were consulted. Enough food and supplies for a long journey were prepared. Gold was provided to trade with faraway peoples in the home of the setting sun.

Griot 3: Abubakari watched as 400 ships set sail from the west coast of Africa. He waited for their return. And he waited. Finally, one lone ship returned to say that the rest had sailed off and disappeared to follow the setting sun.

Children: Tell us, wise ones, what did the king do?
Tell us what your fathers told you.

Griot 1: This time Abubakari himself decided to lead his own expedition. Only this time, he spared no expense! A great fleet of 2,000 ships was built and prepared for the fantastic journey.

Griot 2: When all was ready, Abubakari stepped down from his throne. He gave the empire of Mali to his brother. He said good-bye to his beloved land.

Griot 3: Abubakari climbed aboard his royal ship as the leader of the magnificent procession. His majestic fleet sailed down the Senegal River and west across the sea, following the path of the setting sun.

Children: Tell us more. There's so much to learn.
Tell us, please, did they ever return?

Griot 1: Abubakari was never heard from again in the kingdom of Mali. Not a single ship came back. But 200 years later, when Columbus sailed to the Americas, various explorers told amazing stories about communities they found of people living in the Americas who looked as if they were descendants from Africa!

Griot 2: European explorers found gold on the tips of spears that was different from the gold mined in the Americas. This gold was tested, and it was believed to be the same as gold found in Africa!

Griot 3: Over the years, ocean currents were studied. Ships of ancient design were built and tested. Many historians came to believe that it was possible for early explorers—from Africa!—to reach the Americas before Columbus did.

Children: Tell us now. Is there more to know?
Tell us before we have to go.

Griot 1: We've told you our story from beginning to end.
We've told you so you can tell all of your friends.

Griot 2: Tell them of kingdoms of power and gold.
Tell them of scholars and cities of old.

Griot 3: Tell them in ways they will understand.
Tell them that Africa is a glorious land!

Narrator: Some historians think Abubakari's royal fleet reached the Americas in the early 1300s. This would have been nearly 200 years before Columbus. We do not know for sure. But we do know what the griots in Africa say. And they still tell the story of Abubakari today.

Possible Extensions

1. Look at a globe or world map with your students. Discuss various remote regions of the world. Ask students each to choose one region they would like to explore. Provide time to research that region. Then have students make a travel brochure or poster inviting people to join them on an exploring party to visit that particular region of the world.

2. Discuss with students what it might have been like for Abubakari II and the people of Mali to sail from Africa to the Americas in the early 1300s. Invite students to imagine they were on the journey, too. Have them each write a mock diary describing a two-week account of their adventure.

3. Abubakari II prepared his ships with enough supplies to last on a two-year journey. Instruct each student to make a list of supplies they would need to pack for a one-week trip. For homework, have them look online or go to a store and write down the cost of each item on their list. Then have them estimate the total cost for a one-week trip. After sharing their results, have each student then calculate his or her expenses for a two-year journey. Based on their results, estimate the total cost for supplies for the entire class to take a two-year journey together. Discuss whether they would need closer to 400 ships or 2,000 ships for the entire class to join Abubakari's fleet.

   For added interest, make a bar graph of some of the items students included on their lists. For each item on the graph, count the number of students who included that item on their list. When the graph is completed, discuss the results.

4. Have students draw a picture of what Abubakari II might have looked like sailing at the head of his fleet of 2,000 ships. Invite students to look at a picture of Mansa Musa, another wealthy king of Mali, by visiting the Web site: www.digitalhistory.uh.edu/learning _history/1492/1492_timbuktu.cfm.

5. Historians debate whether or not Abubakari II landed successfully in the Americas nearly 200 years before Columbus. Divide students into partners. Have one student from each pair make a list of reasons supporting why Abubakari's voyage might have been a success. Have the second student make a list of reasons denying the possibility. When finished, invite partners to volunteer and debate their different points of view in front of the class. After the debates, ask students to cast their votes to determine on which side of the debate they stand.

The American Revolution

Heroes and Patriots

Staging

The three narrators can stand at a podium, desk, or music stand on the far right of the stage. The three reporters should be standing near each other on the left of the stage. The four soldiers can be sitting on stools in the center of the stage.

Characters

Narrators 1, 2, and 3   Peter Salem
Reporters 1, 2, and 3   Barzillai Lew
Prince Estabrook   Salem Poor

```
                        Peter Salem    Barzillai Lew
                             X              X
        Prince Estabrook                              Salem Poor
             X                                             X

Reporters 1, 2, 3
   X   X   X
                                                    3 Narrators
                                                     X  X  X
```

Note: Before reading the script, explain to students that these four African American patriots actually fought in the American Revolution, even though this is a fictitious interview and they may not have all known each other.

Narrator 1: Boston was an important city in colonial days. When King George III of England taxed the colonists, he ordered British troops to be stationed in Boston. These soldiers, called Redcoats, made sure everyone obeyed the king. The citizens of Boston didn't like the Redcoats staying in their city. On March 5, 1770, a mob of angry colonists argued with a group of Redcoats on the streets of Boston. Shots rang out. Crispus Attucks, a sailor who had once been a slave, and several other men lay dead on the street. This event became known as the Boston Massacre. Tension continued to grow between England and the American colonists. On April 19, 1775, at a town near Boston called Lexington, the Redcoats and the Minutemen fired shots against each other. The American Revolution had begun.

Reporter 1: I'd like to interview one of our brave heroes from the American Revolution. Sir, where were you when the war began?

Prince Estabrook: I'm from Lexington, so I had signed up to be a Minuteman to protect our town. When Paul Revere rode through the countryside on his famous ride, we heard the British soldiers were coming. I grabbed my gun. I joined the other Minutemen on Lexington Green. We were ready when the Redcoats came marching down the road, even though they had many more soldiers than we did.

Reporter 2: Why did you want to be a Minuteman?

Prince Estabrook: I had once been a slave. But now I knew what it was like to be free. The king of England sometimes treated the colonists as if they were his slaves and had to do anything he demanded. This would not do! All people were created equal, and every person should be free.

Reporter 3: Reports say that you were wounded. Is this true?

Prince Estabrook: Yes, I was listed among the wounded that day. Others died. I was willing to die, too, for liberty from the king. I was also hoping that this war would end slavery in America.

Reporter 1: After the short battle on Lexington Green, the British soldiers marched on to Concord. I'd like to interview another brave hero from the American Revolution. Sir, can you describe that day at Concord?

Peter Salem: On that same day, the British marched on to Concord to try and destroy our supplies. When I heard the Redcoats were coming, I joined the Minutemen gathering at the Concord Bridge. We fought the British troops there.

Reporter 2: Was this the only fighting you saw during the war?

Peter Salem: I fought at Concord, the Battle of Bunker Hill, and many other important battles throughout the war. I had been a slave, but I was given my freedom so that I could become a soldier.

Reporter 3: What happened after the battle at Concord Bridge?

Peter Salem: The Redcoats knew they had to get back to Boston before dark. British warships were floating in Boston Harbor. The big guns made Boston a safe place for the Redcoats to stay. They weren't safe in Concord. More and more Minutemen were running in from the surrounding countryside to fight.

The British soldiers turned around and headed back to Boston. They burned houses in the towns and villages along the way. I followed them back along the road. Other Minutemen came, too. Together we hid behind rocks and trees. We fired at the troops all the way back to Boston. Many Redcoats were killed and even more were wounded. They weren't going to destroy our towns and our homes without a fight!

Reporter 1: After the Redcoats returned to Boston, Minutemen from towns near and far came and camped just outside the city. The Siege of Boston had begun. Here is another brave Revolutionary War hero who was there for the siege. Tell us, sir, what the siege was like.

Barzillai Lew: By late May, about 16,000 American soldiers were camped outside of Boston. I was there with my regiment, the Twenty-Seventh Massachusetts. Our camps were just far enough away from Boston that the British warships couldn't hit us with their guns. But we were close enough to Boston to make sure those Redcoats couldn't get out of the city. We didn't want them marching through the countryside again, burning our towns or stealing our guns.

Reporter 2: Was this the first time you had ever experienced the life of a soldier?

Barzillai Lew: No, I had also fought in the French and Indian War. I was born free, so I was free to enlist whenever I wanted to fight and defend my country. I'm a soldier, but I also play the fife and the drum. During the Siege of Boston, there really wasn't any fighting going on, so I spent my time practicing my fife. We drilled and marched and built walls of defense against the British. Soldiers were short of gunpowder, short of blankets, and short of food. Some men stole chickens and pigs from nearby farms to survive.

Reporter 3: Did the patriots ever fight the troops in Boston?

Barzillai Lew: About two months after the siege began, the Battle of Bunker Hill took place on June 17, 1775. Just before the battle, one of our spies brought word that the Redcoats were planning to move. The American generals decided to move first and surprise the British before they could attack. Before we took action, our troops marched in a short parade, then prayers were said. Finally, under the secret cover of night, we marched silently to Bunker Hill. I kept my fife at my side, ready to play *Yankee Doodle* to encourage the men during the battle.

Narrator 2: One brave soldier distinguished himself above the rest at the Battle of Bunker Hill. His leadership and fighting abilities were recognized by fourteen officers that day. A petition was written and signed by all fourteen, recommending Salem Poor as the hero of the battle.

Reporter 1: Here with us today is our brave hero. Sir, can you describe what happened?

Salem Poor: All night long, we worked hard to build a fort and walls of earth and stone near Bunker's Hill, overlooking Boston. When the sun came up, the British warships were shocked! Here in just one night, they could see that the Americans had taken over the hill.

Reporter 2: What happened next?

Salem Poor: Those warships started to fire their cannons at us. All of Boston woke up. Soon the Redcoats gathered along the water's edge at Boston. They crossed the water by boat, landed their men, and marched up our hill. Two times they advanced up to our fort, but we shot them back. The third time, though, most of our soldiers had run out of ammunition. The Redcoats pushed their way into our fort. The fighting was fierce.

Reporter 3: After you became a hero in this battle, did you leave the army?

Salem Poor: No, I was also at Valley Forge. Along with many others, I experienced that long, cold winter with George Washington. We were fighting for freedom and liberty—for America and for the slaves who suffered in chains.

Narrator 3: About 5,000 African Americans fought in the American Revolution. Black patriots fought both on land and on sea, and in many battles during the war. Because of these brave heroes and others like them, America won the war against England. Their efforts did not bring an end to slavery, however, as so many had hoped it would. It would take another hundred years and another war, the Civil War, before slavery would officially come to an end in America.

Possible Extensions

1. Make a Wall of Fame honoring African American patriots in the American Revolution. Assign each student a different patriot's name to research from William C. Nell's *The Colored Patriots of the American Revolution.* (Available for free download at http://docsouth.unc.edu/neh/nell/nell.html.) On matching sheets of paper, have students each write a one-page biography of the patriots they are studying. Mount these together on the Wall of Fame. Search the Internet to find portraits of various patriots such as Lemuel Haynes, James Forten, and Prince Whipple. Print out as many portraits as possible, or invite students to illustrate portraits on their own, and add these to the Wall of Fame.

2. Students may enjoy viewing two primary source documents about African American patriots in the American Revolution at these Web sites:

   • **Prince Estabrook** (also known as Easterbrooks): http://www.pbs.org/wgbh/aia/part2/2h2.html

   • **Peter Salem:** http://www.nps.gov/bost/planyourvisit/upload/Salem%20Poor%202-14-01.pdf

3. There are two famous illustrations of Peter Salem and the Battle of Bunker Hill. One is on page 20 of William C. Nell's *The Colored Patriots of the American Revolution,* available at the following Web site: http://docsouth.unc.edu/neh/nell/nell.html. The second is available at: http://esperstamps.org/aa6.htm. Show students both illustrations. Compare and contrast the two, discussing the different artists' point of view. Explain that historical events can appear differently in different accounts because they are presented through the eyes and personal background of the author or artist who portrays that event. Invite students to illustrate their own picture of when Peter Salem fought at Bunker Hill.

4. Barzillai Lew's family went on to distinguish themselves in the military. Generations of Lew's descendents served their country from colonial days on up to modern times, including the Civil War and both World Wars. Invite your students to interview their own relatives and create a family tree of their current family members as well as ancestors who served in the United States military.

5. For more information about Barzillai Lew and his descendents, invite students to explore the following books:

   American Patriots by Gail Buckley (New York: Random House, 2001).

   Soldiers of Freedom by Kai Wright (New York: Black Dog & Leventhal Publishers, 2002).

   Twenty Families of Color in Massachusetts by Franklin A. Dorman (Boston: New England Historic Genealogical Society, 1998).

6. Discuss with students about the issue of slavery during the American Revolution. Ask them to share opinions about why they think many colonists, both black and white, hoped this war might bring an end to slavery in America. Compare the history of slavery in England with the history of slavery in America during the years that the Revolutionary War took place.

Founding Fathers

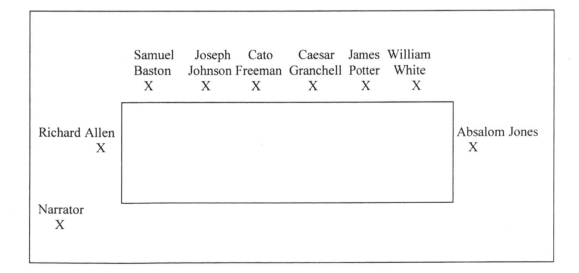

Richard Allen and the Free African Society

Staging

Seat all eight characters around a long table with six along one side so they are facing the audience. Seat Richard Allen at the head of the table on the left and Absalom Jones at the opposite end of the table on the right. The narrator may stand at a podium, desk, or music stand at the far left of the stage. If desired, dress characters in colonial-style clothing.

Characters

Narrator
Richard Allen
Absalom Jones
Samuel Baston
Joseph Johnson

Cato Freeman
Caesar Granchell
James Potter
William White

	Samuel Baston	Joseph Johnson	Cato Freeman	Caesar Granchell	James Potter	William White	
	X	X	X	X	X	X	
Richard Allen X							Absalom Jones X
Narrator X							

Narrator: During the early years of our nation, Philadelphia was a very important city. The Liberty Bell rang out with news of important events. The State House was there. Today it is known as Independence Hall. This was where the Declaration of Independence was written. From 1790 to 1800, Philadelphia was the capital city of the United States of America.

During this time, Philadelphia was also the home of the largest community of free blacks in the nation. The city was a gateway to the North along the Underground Railroad. Many runaway slaves experienced their first taste of freedom when they arrived in Philadelphia. Former slave Richard Allen became known as a powerful Methodist preacher in the years following the American Revolution. In 1786, he was invited to move to Philadelphia and preach to the black congregation of St. George's Methodist Church. When he arrived in this important city, he saw free African Americans struggling to find jobs. He saw many dealing with racial injustices. Because of racism, they couldn't get a good education. Richard Allen stepped forward as a leader of Philadelphia's community of free blacks. He helped in any way he could.

Richard Allen: Last month on April 12, 1787, my good friend Absalom Jones and I met. We discussed our deep concerns about our fellow Africans. Here in Philadelphia exists the largest group of free blacks living in the United States. Yet our hearts are filled with sorrow. Everywhere we look, our brothers and sisters are living without churches and without opportunities for a good education. Many of us have escaped the chains of slavery or bought our freedom as Absalom and I did. Even so, most free blacks still suffer from overwhelming hardships.

Absalom Jones: After much serious discussion last month, Richard Allen and I decided to form a society. This society would not be connected with any church. Each of us has our own religious preferences. However, members of this society must agree to live a respectable and honest life. Members will also help each other through times of sickness. We will also help widows and fatherless children. When we met together last month, Richard and I decided to write down these ideas. Together, we wrote the Preamble for a Free African Society.

Narrator: The first monthly meeting of the Free African Society took place at an important time in the history of America. Allen, Jones, and the other six members of this new society met in Philadelphia on May 17, 1787. Just down the street from them, the Constitutional Convention was getting ready to start. Delegates from all over the new nation were arriving at Independence Hall. They planned to write the laws and the Constitution for our country. George Washington had arrived in Philadelphia for the Convention just four days earlier. The Constitutional Convention was scheduled to start on May 25. Let's join the following eight men. This is a fictionalized account of the actual historic event of the very first meeting of the Free African Society.

Richard Allen: This is our first general meeting. Let's have a discussion about the rules and guidelines for our society. We, the free Africans and our families, of the City of Philadelphia, in the State of Pennsylvania, or elsewhere, should all agree on these guidelines.

Samuel Baston: Without money to support our efforts, we will not be able to accomplish much good. It is reasonable for each one of us to agree to pay one shilling in silver Pennsylvania currency each month. After one year from today's date, we should then have enough money in our treasury. We will be able to help the poor and needy. Of course, we will make sure they are not in need of money because they have been doing bad things.

Joseph Johnson: We should also set guidelines about new members who want to join our society. No drunkard or disorderly person should be allowed to become a member. And if someone does join our society and then later on becomes disorderly, he should have to give up his membership. He will not get any of his money back.

Cato Freeman: If any member doesn't pay his monthly dues, then after three months, we should tell him about it. If he doesn't pay the whole amount by the next meeting, he should have to give up his membership. He will not get any of his money back. That is unless, of course, he has a good reason that he is not able to make payments at that time.

Caesar Granchell: Also, if any member is absent for the monthly meeting, he should be required to pay three pence unless he is sick. No man can work and earn a wage when he is sick. He would not have to pay his monthly dues or fines until he is strong enough to go back to work and return to the meetings.

James Potter: If a member of our society dies, we should help his widow and children. The widow should enjoy all the benefits of this society. She should not have to pay the monthly dues. The children should be protected under our care, especially regarding their education. If they cannot attend the free school, we should help them find suitable work or places to become an apprentice.

William White: The way we handle our money is important. No one member should be allowed to spend money or transact business except by approval given at a monthly meeting or by a committee. All money should be handled by the Clerk and Treasurer. It should be always understood that one of the people called Quakers should be chosen for this useful Institution.

Richard Allen: Your assistance and useful remarks are truly helpful. Do we all agree on these Articles for the Free African Society?

All: Agreed.

Richard Allen: Then I will mark down that this evening the articles were read. After some remarks were made, they were agreed unto.

Narrator: So it was that the Free African Society was formed in Philadelphia. The Preamble and its Articles were written. Scholar and historian W.E.B. Du Bois said that even though we may not realize it, this meeting was one of the most important steps a group of people ever took.

These men overcame tremendous odds. They rose up out of the chains of slavery. There were no other footsteps for them to follow. Richard Allen and other black Founding Fathers established societies and founded churches. They opened schools. They worked hard to help free blacks living in America. They could not attend the meetings at Independence Hall—those doors were closed to people of color. So they met together just down the street from the nation's new government. They inspired black leaders in other cities to step forward to follow their courageous example.

Possible Extensions

1. To read the Preamble and Articles of the Free African Society, have students visit the following Web site: http://www.pbs.org/wgbh/aia/part3/3h465.html.

2. The Richard Allen Museum at Mother Bethel A.M.E. Church in Philadelphia has a Web site featuring an in-depth look at the history of Africans in America as well as Richard Allen's important contributions as a black Founding Father. Students may visit the museum's Web site at: http://www.motherbethel.org/museum/.

3. Students may wish to form a club to discuss new ways to help meet the particular needs of students at their school. Have them discuss and draw up a set of guidelines for the club.

4. Philadelphia had the largest community of free blacks in the early years of our nation because it was the gateway to freedom along the Underground Railroad. Students may want to investigate more about the fugitive slaves who arrived in Philadelphia. Direct them to read portions of William Still's book, *The Underground Railroad: A Record of Facts, Authentic Narratives, Letters, &c., Narrating the Hardships, Hair-Breadth Escapes and Death Struggles of the Slaves in Their Efforts for Freedom, As Related by Themselves and Others, or Witnessed by the Author.* This book is available for free download at the Web site: http://www.gutenberg.org/etext/15263.

5. Invite students to create their own script about fugitive slaves arriving in Philadelphia. They may choose an example from William Still's book *The Underground Railroad* to use as a guide while they write.

Abolitionists

Robert and Harriet (Forten) Purvis Help Lead the Fight

Staging

Seat the first three characters, Harriet Purvis, Robert Purvis, and William Lloyd Garrison, in a group at the center of the stage to appear as if they are sitting together in the Purvis home. Include two empty chairs for James and Charlotte Forten to join them later. The narrator may stand at the front of the stage. James and Charlotte Forten, along with the messenger, may wait off stage until their turn to speak.

Characters

Narrator   Messenger
William Lloyd Garrison   Charlotte Forten
Harriet Purvis   James Forten
Robert Purvis

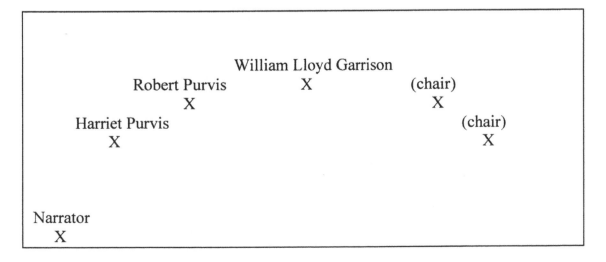

Narrator: In the years before the Civil War, on one of the beautiful tree-lined streets of Philadelphia, Pennsylvania, we find a handsome and well-built house. It is owned by a wealthy African American family of abolitionists, people who believe slavery should come to an end. Today a friend from Boston is visiting. Let's listen to the imaginary conversation of these real people who worked closely together to help in the fight against slavery.

William Lloyd Garrison: Thank you so much, dear friends, for inviting me to visit your lovely home here in the city of brotherly love.

Harriet Purvis: We are honored with your visit, Mr. Garrison. We are hoping soon to purchase an estate just out of the city. We plan to raise some of the finest horses and livestock in the area.

William Lloyd Garrison: What an honorable livelihood that will be! I'm sure your animals will take first place at all the local fairs.

Robert Purvis: Thank you. We are hoping to set an example to others to take pride in their labors.

Harriet Purvis: We also support the Free Produce Society.

William Lloyd Garrison: How does that work?

Robert Purvis: We purchase only fruits and vegetables from local farms sold at the market. We do not purchase any product—not even cotton—from a plantation that owns slaves.

Harriet Purvis: If everyone bought their food and cotton from the Free Produce Society, the plantations would not get any money. Perhaps that would help them decide to free their slaves and hire them as workers instead. Then we would buy food from their farms, too.

Narrator: Just then they heard a knock at the door.

Messenger: Excuse me, Mr. and Mrs. Purvis. I have a letter to you from Mr. William Still.

Robert Purvis:	Thank you. Please allow me to read the letter aloud: *A slave catcher has just arrived in town on the boat at the dock. He says he is looking for a family with a mother, father, and two small children. They have run away from a plantation in South Carolina.*
Harriet Purvis:	That sounds like the family we are hiding in our secret room.
Robert Purvis:	I was planning on taking them to the train depot today and buying them all tickets to Canada.
Harriet Purvis:	With that slave catcher in town, though, they would not be safe at the train. He would capture them and take them back to slavery!
Narrator:	Robert Purvis quickly wrote William Still a letter. He handed it to the messenger.
Robert Purvis:	Take this letter to Mr. Still at once. It says we will not move our packages until we receiver further instructions from him.
Messenger (leaving):	Yes, sir.
William Lloyd Garrison:	Do you help many on their way to freedom?
Harriet Purvis:	Yes. As part of the Underground Railroad here in Philadelphia, many fugitives stay in our shelter. We give them food and clothes. We buy them tickets north to Canada where they will be safe from the slave catchers who hunt them down.
Robert Purvis:	Philadelphia is one of the busiest stops on the Underground Railroad. It's often the first city where fugitives who are escaping from slave states in the South land on free soil. William Still documents every person's story who comes through our city.
Harriet Purvis:	Just the other day, a most unusual event occurred. Mr. Still was talking with a man who had just escaped from slavery in the South. He listened to this man's description of his mother, father, and brother who had been separated from him as a child. Suddenly Mr. Still realized he was speaking face to

face with his own, dear brother! The cruelties of slavery had separated them many years ago, but now Providence brought them back together again. It made me weep to hear of it.

Narrator: A fancy carriage pulled up in front of the house. An elderly couple got out, dressed in elegant fashion and style. They walked into the house. There was no need to knock.

Harriet Purvis: Mother! Father! What a nice surprise to see you here today. Come sit with us and our guest.

Charlotte Forten: Good day, Mr. Garrison! What a pleasure to experience your company on our visit today.

James Forten: I trust you received my recent letter to you?

William Lloyd Garrison: Yes. Truly I thank you for your many generous subscriptions and donations. Without your support, *The Liberator* would not be the newspaper it is today. But tell me, when most free blacks in our society today are as poor and penniless as I am, a poor white man, how is it that your family acquired its great wealth?

James Forten: When I was a youth living in Philadelphia, I was poor enough. That was during the Revolutionary War. I signed up and served as a powder boy on a small ship. I carried powder to the men to fire off the ship's cannons. The British Navy captured our vessel, and I became a prisoner of war on that terrible prison ship, the *Jersey*. I was one of the few to survive its horrors. Finally set free, I returned to Philadelphia and worked for a company making sails. After years of hard work, I bought the company myself.

Charlotte Forten: All our sons have worked in our sail loft, too. With so many tall ships in and out of port, we have a busy and prosperous business. But that is not how our dear Robert got his money.

Robert Purvis: My father was a wealthy Englishman who moved to South Carolina and sold cotton. My mother's ancestors were from Africa's shores. While yet young, my brother and I moved to Philadelphia to attend school. It is here that we became dear friends with the Forten family.

James Forten: When Robert's father died, he and his brother became like my own sons. They both inherited his great fortune.

Charlotte Forten: By then, both young men had fallen in love with two of our daughters. We are fortunate to have them be such an important part of our family.

William Lloyd Garrison: Your entire family is involved in the fight against slavery, is it not?

Harriet Purvis: Yes, Mother and I, along with my sisters, have helped found the Philadelphia Female Anti-Slavery Society. We hold many fairs to raise money to assist fugitives on their way north. We are frequently invited to lecture to persuade people to take a stand for equal rights and bring slavery to an end.

James Forten: Robert and I often work together. We are members and also leaders of different Anti-Slavery societies. We lecture as well as write petitions, letters of protest, and newspaper articles. Every member of our family believes in the equality of all people.

William Lloyd Garrison: I frequently publish well-written articles and poems in *The Liberator* that come from the pen of your sons and daughters as well as yourself, Mr. Forten.

James Forten: Yes, we support your paper as much as possible.

Robert Purvis: Our efforts today are also aimed against the Colonization Society. This society has presidential support as well as the support of wealthy plantation owners from the South. These men are trying to get rid of free blacks like ourselves and force us to move back to Africa.

James Forten: We are Americans! My friends and I fought for our freedom in the American Revolution. We will not allow anyone to force us to leave our home and the land we love, even with all its sorrows and troubles.

Charlotte Forten: If we were forced to move to Africa, who would help our brothers and sisters who are still suffering here in the chains of slavery?

Harriet Purvis: We must continue to dedicate our lives to help our country bring an end to this dark stain of slavery.

Narrator: Harriet and Robert Purvis, along with James and Charlotte Forten, continued to lead the fight against slavery. Their efforts were not wasted. Finally, the Civil War broke out between the North and the South. Harriet and Robert's niece, Charlotte Forten (named after Harriet's mother) was a teacher to freed slaves on the South Carolina Sea Islands during the war. Their son, Charles Purvis, enlisted as a surgeon in the army. After the war was over and slavery came to an end, Charles Purvis became the first African American to oversee a hospital when he was appointed as surgeon-in-chief of Freedman's Hospital in Washington, D.C. This famous family of black abolitionists from Philadelphia truly helped establish America as the land of the free.

Possible Extensions

1. Videotape your students' performance of this readers theatre performance. Share it with other classes to help increase awareness about the important work abolitionists did during the years before the Civil War.

2. Make a word search for students using the names of the following black abolitionists, well known and influential in their day. After students have found all the names on the word search, have them research different people from the list. Allow time to share with the class about each abolitionist's efforts to fight against slavery.

   Robert Purvis, Harriet Purvis, James Forten, Charles Remond, Sarah Remond, Richard Allen, Prince Hall, William Whipper, John Langston, William Wells Brown, Absalom Jones, Samuel Ward, Abraham Shadd, Mary Ann Shadd Cary, Frances Harper, William Nell, Maria Stewart, Henry Garnet, Jermain Loguen, William Still, Martin Delany, John Jones, Frederick Douglass, Lewis Hayden, Sojourner Truth

3. Many abolitionists lectured frequently to persuade people to join the fight against slavery. Divide students into small groups. Assign each group a topic from local, national, or worldwide current events. Have members of each group discover more about their topic in the news. Encourage them to discuss the topic with their parents or other informed adults. Invite guests to your class to speak on each topic. After students are familiar with the current event their group is studying, have each one write a lecture to present to the class to persuade others to support his or her opinion about it.

4. Robert and Harriet Purvis could not see into the future to predict the outcome of all their hard work as abolitionists. They did not know there would be a Civil War, segregation laws, or a Civil Rights Movement. Choose one current event to discuss with your students. Invite them to predict what will happen in 10 years, 50 years, and 100 years concerning this issue.

5. Locate the city of Philadelphia on a map. Discuss why it was an important station on the Underground Railroad. (It was a busy seaport, trains stopped there frequently, and the free state of Pennsylvania bordered slave states.) To view different routes of the Underground Railroad, invite your students to visit the following Web sites:

   • http://education.ucdavis.edu/NEW/STC/lesson/socstud/railroad/Map.htm

   • http://americanabolitionist.liberalarts.iupui.edu/ugrr.htm

   • http://undergroundrailroadconductor.com/

6. Robert Purvis and other abolitionists wrote petitions and gathered signatures to send to government leaders in hopes of improving conditions for free African Americans as well as those who were enslaved. Brainstorm with your students to discuss a short list of positive changes that could be made to improve your school or community. Together as a class, choose one item and write a petition recommending this improvement. Encourage students to collect signatures for the petition and submit it to the principal, school board, or community leaders.

The Black Press

The North Star Shines a Bright Light

Staging

Seat Frederick Douglass and Martin Delany at a table so they are facing the audience. Give both characters a newspaper to hold on the table. If possible, change the title of the newspapers to be *The North Star*. Two narrators may stand at the front left of the stage. The other two narrators may stand at the front right. All remaining characters should wait offstage until it is their turn. They should then walk onstage, stand at the side of the table, speak their part, and then exit offstage when they are done.

Characters

Narrators 1, 2, 3, and 4   Henry Highland Garnet
William Cooper Nell   Charles Remond
Frederick Douglass   Sarah Parker Remond
Martin Delany

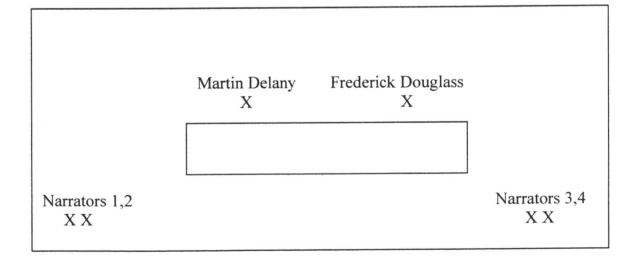

Narrator 1: Martin Delany was of direct African descent. His mother was free, so he was born free even though his father was enslaved. Laws of the time stated that if a mother was free, her children were born free. If she was a slave, her children were born slaves as well.

Narrator 2: Delany grew up and moved to Pittsburgh, where he became a leader of the city's anti-slavery society as well as many literary, temperance, and self-improvement societies in the area.

Narrator 1: Continuing his education at night school, he also received training to be a doctor. For the rest of his life, Martin Delany practiced medicine. He married Catherine Richards, and together they had seven children. They named each child after famous African American leaders throughout history such as Toussaint L'Ouverture and Alexander Dumas.

Narrator 2: From around 1843 until 1847, Martin Delany published the newspaper known as *The Mystery*. He eventually joined with Frederick Douglass to co-edit *The North Star*. Frederick Douglass once said of him, "I thank God for making me a man, but Delany always thanks God for making him a *black* man." In an era when many people looked down upon African Americans, Martin Delany was proud of his heritage and who he was.

Narrator 3: Frederick Douglass was born into slavery in Maryland. As a child, he suffered from cold and hunger, and his mother died when he was young. Too young to do heavy work, Frederick Douglass did chores and ran errands until he was old enough to become a house slave. He was sent to work in the home of his master's relative in Baltimore.

Narrator 4: It was in Baltimore where Frederick Douglass learned to read and write. Eventually, however, he was sent back to the plantation. At sixteen, he was hired out to work on a different farm under a master who was known as a "slave breaker." Whipped often, Frederick Douglass fought back. He tried to escape but was discovered and locked up in jail.

Narrator 3: Frederick Douglass was later hired out to work in Baltimore shipyards. In this city, he met free blacks, including his future wife, Anna Murray. Anna helped Frederick plan his escape. He dressed up as a sailor and borrowed a free man's papers on his journey to escape from the slave state of Maryland to the free state of New York.

Narrator 4: Frederick Douglass began reading William Lloyd Garrison's abolitionist newspaper, *The Liberator.* Hearing Douglass lecture at an anti-slavery meeting he was attending, the Anti-Slavery Society asked him to become one of their agents. He toured for several years as one of their speakers and eventually published his autobiography in 1845. The publication of his book endangered his freedom, so he traveled to speak in England where he would be safe from the slave catchers. Once there, funds were raised to purchase his freedom and help him start his own newspaper. Frederick Douglass returned to Rochester, New York, where he joined with Martin Delany to co-edit *The North Star.* Join us in this fictitious scene where actual famous black abolitionists of the day visit the two editors to discuss the new paper.

William Cooper Nell: Good day, gentlemen! I see you have the very first issue of *The North Star* in front of you. How does it look? What do you think?

Frederick Douglass: I think we were right when we decided to call it *The North Star.* The title is so bold and bright at the top of the paper. Just like the North Star guides the escaping slaves north through the night on their journey to freedom, this paper will be a shining light to guide Americans on our journey to bring freedom to the slaves.

Martin Delany: Already, people are signing up for subscriptions. This newspaper will keep the black community on top of current news regarding our rights as citizens of America. We'll print parts of people's speeches who lecture about bringing an end of slavery. We'll print articles encouraging everyone, both black and white, to take a stand against slavery. What's your opinion, Nell, as the publisher of *The North Star*? What do you think of our first issue?

William Cooper Nell: This first issue is all I'd hoped it would be. I'm excited to be part of this great new enterprise. Delany, with your past knowledge of publishing your own paper, *The Mystery,* you'll bring a strong background and wise measure of experience to this project. Douglass, with your circle of friends that include well-known abolitionist leaders both black and white, this paper is sure to be a success.

Martin Delany: We need to get a strong subscription base to have the finances to continue publishing this paper. I'm planning on traveling and lecturing to let the public know about *The North Star.* I'll encourage people to subscribe. I'll also keep my ears open for any news we might want to include.

Frederick Douglass: Many of our friends are planning to write articles to contribute. Politics and the power of the pen will be an effective way to fight against slavery.

William Cooper Nell: I hope you're right, Douglass. Time will tell. I believe in the power of the pen, too. That's why I write all the pamphlets, articles, and books that I do. But it's time for me to go now. I'll see you tomorrow.

Martin Delany and Frederick Douglass: Good-bye.

(William Cooper Nell exits, and Henry Highland Garnet enters.)

Henry Highland Garnet: Congratulations on the publication of your newspaper! I pray it will be an instrument used in the hands of God to help ease the suffering of so many of our brothers and sisters in bondage.

Martin Delany: Since you are the pastor of the Liberty Street Church, we were thinking it would be a good idea to print some of your sermons in the pages of *The North Star.*

Frederick Douglass: Yes, this would make your teachings available to a great number of Americans and not just the ones who are able to hear you preach. What do you think of the idea?

Henry Highland Garnet: I would be honored to have my words printed in your paper. Unfortunately, I know you do not always agree with my opinion. I believe in resistance. Resistance is the only way slaves will overcome their situation and break the chains of slavery! In spite of our differences, however, I think your paper will be a great success. I would appreciate having my viewpoints expressed within its pages. Good day, sirs, and good-bye!

Martin Delany and Frederick Douglass: Good-bye.

(*Henry Highland Garnet exits, and Charles and Sarah Parker Remond enter.*)

Charles Remond: Hello, gentlemen. I rejoice to see your newspaper finally in print. My sister and I read every word this morning.

Sarah Parker Remond: Yes, it will give me much news to talk about when I speak to abolitionists in England during my tour overseas.

Martin Delany: You both speak so frequently and to such large crowds of people that it would be helpful to have your names joined with *The North Star.*

Frederick Douglass: Your speaking schedules are no doubt full since you both are frequently sought after for lecturing at important events. Do you think you can find time to let your audiences know about *The North Star* and its mission to advance the cause of freedom among all people, black and white, men and women?

Sarah Parker Remond: Of course! I know you support women's suffrage and equal rights as well as the equality of rights for all races. I gladly give my support to *The North Star*.

Charles Remond: And so do I. My sister and I will also use our influence as leaders of the many different anti-slavery societies we're involved in. Together we must work to bring about equal rights among all people. Even free blacks cannot live as full citizens in America. Too many unfair laws oppress us. Laws take away our right to vote, our children's rights to an equal education, and our right to travel, live, and work as we please. My sister and I will continue to lecture in support of the equality of all Americans. We are hoping that your newspaper will reach the hearts and minds of those who are not able to hear us speak.

Martin Delany and Frederick Douglass: Good day, then.

Charles Remond: Good day, sirs!

Sarah Parker Remond: And good-bye.

(Charles and Sarah Parker Remond exit.)

Narrator 1: *The North Star* continued to be a strong voice crying out "Freedom for the slave!" and "Equal rights among those who are free!" Eventually, Frederick Douglass became sole editor of the newspaper. Martin Delany and William Cooper Nell took other important positions in the fight against slavery even though they continued to contribute articles to the paper.

Narrator 2: The passage of the Fugitive Slave Act of 1850 changed the way of life for many. Slave catchers were now permitted and legally supported to move freely throughout northern cities in search of any former slave living a life of freedom. Martin Delany moved his family north to Canada. He led an exploring party in Africa in hopes of establishing a colony of free blacks on Africa's shores. With the outbreak of the Civil War, however, Martin Delany moved back to the United States. President Lincoln commissioned him as a major in the U.S. Army. He recruited black troops and served in South Carolina.

Narrator 3: Frederick Douglass also recruited black troops, including his own sons for the famous 54th Massachusetts Regiment. He devoted much of his energy and thought into discussing important issues with President Lincoln. After the end of the war, Frederick Douglass remained politically active. He served in various government appointments including as a minister to Haiti.

Narrator 4: Martin Delany was a doctor, editor, writer, speaker, and officer in the army. He was also one of the most important abolitionists of all during the years leading up to the Civil War. Frederick Douglass escaped from slavery and rose up to become one of the most famous speakers, writers, and influential leaders our nation has ever known.

Possible Extensions

1. Invite students to read actual articles that appeared in *The North Star* by visiting the following Web site: www.dalnet.lib.mi.us. Click on the link for "Digital Projects." Then click on the link for "Black Abolitionist Archive." Next click on the link for "Newspapers." Click on the link for "N-O." Then click on the link for "North Star." Follow the links to read any of the eighteen articles listed. To view an actual issue of this historic newspaper, direct students to the Web site: www.americaslibrary.gov/ cgi-bin/page.cgi/aa/activists/douglass/leader_1.

2. In the years leading up to the Civil War, different African American leaders held differing views on how to bring an end to slavery. Henry Highland Garnet believed in resistance and the use of force or violent action. William Cooper Nell believed in the power of persuading people to make the choice that slavery was an evil part of society. Martin Delany believed in emigration—moving away from America to countries where slavery didn't exist such as Canada, Jamaica, or Liberia. Frederick Douglass believed in politics and electing political leaders who would defend every citizen's constitutional rights. Discuss each of these viewpoints with your students. Ask them each to choose one viewpoint to support and write a newspaper article for a classroom version of *The North Star*. Have them each list three reasons in their article supporting why they believe their viewpoint would work to bring an end to slavery.

3. Engage a discussion with students about current issues in the world today such as world hunger or military dictatorship. Based on the four differing viewpoints of Garnet, Nell, Delany, and Douglass, ask each student to choose one method to solve the problem. Invite volunteers to debate why they think their method would work best.

4. Martin Delany and his wife, Catherine, were proud of their heritage as African Americans. They named each of their children after names of historic leaders of African descent including the following names: Toussaint L'Ouverture, Charles Lenox Remond, Alexandre Dumas, Saint Cyprian, Faustin Soulouque, and Placido Rameses. (Note that one son was named after both Cuba's romantic poet Placido and the Egyptian pharaoh Ramses the Great.) Together with your students, look up the biographies of as many of these names as you can find to understand better why the Delanys named their children after these famous people. When finished, encourage students to explore their own cultural heritage. Challenge them to find at least two names of influential men and women who share the same cultural background that they do, whose names they might use if they decided to name their children after them. Have students write a short biography of each person to share with the class and explain why they might choose their names.

5. Before Frederick Douglass became a speaker for the Anti-Slavery Society, Charles Lenox Remond was one of the most famous black abolitionist speakers in this era. Discuss details about both Remond's and Douglass's lives. Draw a Venn diagram on the board and use it to organize data to compare and contrast the similarities and differences between these two important leaders.

Settling the West

Bass Reeves Keeps the Law

Staging

The narrators can sit on stools at one side of the stage. During each scene, the characters in that scene should stand in a loose-knit group, move around as they speak, or position themselves as seems best from the dialogue. Characters not in a scene should wait offstage for their turn. Scene 1 begins with Bass Reeves and Campbell standing talking together in the middle of the stage.

Characters

Narrators 1 and 2   Mother
Campbell   First brother
Bass Reeves   Second brother

Bass Reeves X	Campbell X
Narrators 1,2 X X	

Narrator 1: Bass Reeves was the first African American United States Deputy Marshall west of the Mississippi. Born a slave, he grew up in Texas. It's said that during the Civil War, he got in a fight with his owner and ran away. He lived the life of a fugitive until Emancipation came.

Narrator 2: After the Civil War, the West was a rugged land. No place, however, was as wild and dangerous as the area known as Indian Territory. Notorious outlaws from all over the map fled to Indian Territory to escape the law. It was a rough wilderness where men hid out in caves or perched lookouts high on cliffs to keep a watch for any lawman riding by.

Narrator 1: It took courage, it took guts, and it took a man of strong character to sign up to patrol this land. It was just north of Texas. Eventually it became the state of Oklahoma. One man—one of the most famous heroes of the Wild, Wild West—made it his duty and his job to keep the law. This man was Bass Reeves.

Narrator 2: Let's join U.S. Marshal Bass Reeves now in the following scenes. The people in these scenes are real. The script is based on Bass Reeves's legendary capture of two brothers who were running from the law.

Scene 1

Wagon camp in the Indian Territory, just north of the Texas border

Campbell: Do you really think you can catch these two outlaws, Marshal?

Bass Reeves: I'm studying on it. Every day we've camped here with our wagon of supplies, I've been out studying the land. I figure we're about twenty-eight miles away from the cabin of the outlaws' mother. Folks talk, and talk is that these two brothers always hole up at their mother's.

Campbell: That $5,000 reward money sure looks pretty. If you bring them in, I'll help keep guard over them in between times I'm cooking our grub. How do you aim on catching them two rascals?

Bass Reeves: I've given it a lot of thought. Sometimes a disguise works best.

Campbell: You always were one to come up with some fancy disguises! Cowboy, gunfighter, drifter, or horse thief. Which one are you gonna do this time?

Bass Reeves: I figure the best disguise to wear this far out in Indian Territory is to be a drifter. I aim to cut the heels off some old boots I have.

Campbell: That will make it look like you've been walking all the way and don't got no horse. You know the first thing these outlaws look for is the horse. Every marshal rides such a fine one.

Bass Reeves: That's why I'm leaving my horse here with the wagon and going on foot. I also want to make it look like I'm running from the law. I'll shoot three bullet holes in an old hat I have.

Campbell: But if they see your six shooter or your handcuffs, they'll know you're a lawman yourself!

Bass Reeves: I'll hide everything under the loose, raggedy clothes I wear. Even my badge. By the time I walk all the way out to that cabin, I'll be so hot and dirty and wore out, they'll think I'm a drifter all right.

Narrator 1: Bass Reeves got his disguise ready, put on his old hat and boots, and took off heading south. He walked mile after dusty mile. By the time he found the little cabin hideout, he looked like he'd been lost in the Indian Territory for days.

Scene 2

Run-down cabin next to a creek in Indian Territory

Mother: Hey mister! You just stop there in your tracks and don't come no closer to my cabin. State your business. What are you doing all the way out here in the middle of nowhere?

Bass Reeves: I'm running from the law. I haven't had a drip of water for miles. I haven't had a bite to eat for two days. They're hard on my trail. I'm a desperate man.

Mother: You do look a sight for sore eyes. Your lips are cracked and dry. Your clothes are nothing but rags. You're covered with dust and caked with mud from head to foot. Even your old hat is filled with holes.

Bass Reeves: Those holes are from the lawmen's guns. That shows how close they were to ending my life. I'm running from the law, and I'm running hard.

Mother: I know how that is. It sets hard on a man. My own two sons are running from the law. I'll tell you what. Why don't you get yourself a long, cold drink from our well? I'll fix you something to eat.

Bass Reeves: Much obliged, ma'am.

Mother: In fact, I think we should join together. We'll be safer from the law if we hide out together.

Bass Reeves: I couldn't agree with you more.

Narrator 2: After the marshal got a cold drink and a warm meal, he was ready to wait. He didn't have to wait long. Soon it was dark. They heard a whistle from outside the cabin.

Two brothers, from offstage: (*Whistle*)

Mother: Come in sons! It's alright. We have a visitor, but he's on our side.

First brother: We won't come inside the cabin if there's someone else here.

Second brother: How can we trust him and us with an award on our heads?

Mother: No, really! He's running from the law just like you are. He was a sight when he got here, too. I could tell he's been out here in the territory for days. Heels clean wore off of his boots and bullet holes in his hat.

First brother: If you're sure …

Mother: I'm sure! Come on inside the cabin, sons. Have something to eat.

Second brother: I am mighty hungry. All right. If you're sure.

Narrator 1: The two men came into the cabin and got something to eat.

Mother: I've invited our visitor to join us. With greater numbers we'll stand more of a chance.

First brother: Only if he sleeps out in the barn tonight.

Second brother: That's right. I still don't trust him.

Bass Reeves: You've no call for alarm. I won't hurt you. But you do need to fear the law. They're hot on my trail. What if they come tonight and try to break into your cabin?

Mother: He's right, sons. We should let him stay the night in here with us. We could use the extra protection if the law shows up tonight.

First brother: Guess so. You good with a six shooter?

Bass Reeves: I'm tolerable.

Second brother: We can all bed down on the floor.

Narrator 2: That night, the four of them spread out on the floor. The marshal pretended to doze. Soon the outlaws and their mother were sound asleep. Marshal Reeves got up and tiptoed to the side of the first brother. Ever so slowly, he reached inside his shirt and brought out a pair of handcuffs. Ever so gently, he put the handcuffs on the outlaw's wrists. Ever so quietly, he picked up the outlaw's pistol and stuffed it in his own belt. Ever so carefully, he did the exact same thing to the other brother. Once they were both handcuffed, the marshal was ready. It wasn't long until the outlaws heard a loud voice.

Bass Reeves: Wake up! This is the United States law!

First brother: Hey! I can't move my hands!

Second brother: Where's my gun?

Bass Reeves: You two are under arrest. Get up! Get a move on! We're heading in to Fort Smith.

Mother: Why you dirty traitor! You tricked us this whole time! Who do you think you are?

Bass Reeves: I'm United States Marshal Bass Reeves, ma'am.

Mother: I've heard of you! You're famous around these parts. They say you bring in whole wagonloads of outlaws at a time. Fifteen—sometimes sixteen of them all at once. Chained together to a log so they can't get away.

First brother: I've seen signs posted about you. Other outlaws wrote signs saying you better stay out of Indian Territory or you're gonna get shot. By them.

Second brother: You're the one they say dresses up in disguises and speaks all the different languages known around these parts.

Bass Reeves: Yep. That's me! But enough about me. You've got an appointment to keep with the law. And I've got some reward money to collect. Get up! Let's get moving.

Narrator 1: That's how U.S. Marshal Bass Reeves captured two of the most sought-after outlaws of the West. He made them walk all twenty-eight miles back to his camp. Campbell kept guard the rest of the way. They took them to Fort Smith and handed them over to Judge Parker.

Narrator 2: Bass Reeves was a legend in his own time. Newspapers carried reports of the amazing ways he tricked and captured the most notorious outlaws of the West. Near the end of his career, when Indian Territory became the state of Oklahoma, Bass Reeves had captured over 3,000 outlaws and brought them to justice. In 1992, he was inducted into the Hall of Great Westerners at the National Cowboy and Western Heritage Museum in Oklahoma City.

Possible Extensions

1. What kind of words could be used to describe Bass Reeves? Legend, brave, smart? Help your students compile a list of adjectives on the board that define this amazing law man. Distribute graph paper and instruct students to make a word search using these words. Remind them to include each word they used in a list at the bottom. When finished, have them exchange with a partner and circle each word they find.

2. To learn more about Bass Reeves and his daring adventures, your students might want to read the following books:

The Black Badge by Paul L. Brady (Los Angeles: Milligan Books, 2005).

Black Gun, Silver Star by Art T. Burton (Lincoln: University of Nebraska Press, 2006).

3. Explain to students that a legend is a story that many people might know but that might not actually be historically accurate. Because so many legends have been told about Bass Reeves, at times it has been hard to separate the truth from fiction. Ask students to write new, original legends about this famous and heroic U.S. Marshal to share with the class. Discuss the difference between accurate historical accounts, legends, and tall tales. As an added option, have students write tall tales about the Wild, Wild West with Bass Reeves portrayed as the hero.

4. There were at least four basic groups of people who lived in or near the Indian Territory while Bass Reeves was a marshal: law men, outlaws, Native Americans, and settlers. Discuss what life might have been like for each group who lived in this part of the West during this time. Ask students to choose which group they would have preferred to be a part of if they lived during that era, and explain their reasons why.

5. The area known as the Indian Territory in the late 1800s eventually became the state of Oklahoma. Have students research this historic area both then and now. Invite them each to prepare two travel brochures—one describing the Indian Territory in the 1890s during the days of Bass Reeves and one describing Oklahoma today. Among other things, have them include information about natural landmarks, populations, transportation, and important forts, towns, and cities.

Civil War

Emancipation Day on the South Carolina Sea Islands

Staging

The narrator stands at a podium, desk, or music stand at the far left of the stage. Harriet Tubman stands just to the right of the narrator. On the far right of the stage, Charlotte Forten sits on a stool. Next to her stands Sergeant Prince Rivers. Standing just behind them are the freedmen—newly freed men, women, and children of any number you wish to use. The boatmen sit on the floor at the back center of the stage. Each of the main characters are real in this fictionalized scene.

Characters

Narrator	Sergeant Prince Rivers
Harriet Tubman	Group of Freedmen
Charlotte Forten	Boatmen

Boatmen
X X X

Freedmen
X X X X X

Sergeant
Prince Rivers
Charlotte Forten   X
X

Narrator   Harriet Tubman
X   X

Narrator: Fort Sumter stood on an island in the harbor of Charleston, South Carolina. Union soldiers held it under their command. On April 12, 1861, the Confederate Army fired on Fort Sumter. Union forces soon surrendered, and the fort was captured by the South. The American Civil War had begun. Not long after that, Union soldiers returned to South Carolina. They landed their boats just south of Charleston on the South Carolina Sea Islands. Southern plantation owners fled from the islands. Union soldiers discovered over 8,000 slaves left behind.

Harriet Tubman: Union soldiers freed the slaves they found on the South Carolina Sea Islands. Different organizations helped the freedmen, or newly freed slaves. Doctors, missionaries, and teachers went to the South Carolina Sea Islands. I volunteered and worked for two years in a hospital there, nursing the sick and the wounded. Clara Barton was there, too, organizing medical supplies and services throughout the islands. The South Carolina Sea Islands were now the headquarters for the Union Army's Department of the South. When I wasn't helping at the hospital, I worked as a spy. It was dangerous work, but I was used to danger. I went with the army on secret missions to plantations near the islands. I led many slaves to freedom, often in the dark of the night.

Narrator: One of the volunteer teachers who went to the South Carolina Sea Islands was a young woman named Charlotte Forten. The members of her family were famous and wealthy free African Americans, all abolitionists from Philadelphia. Charlotte was becoming a famous abolitionist, too.

Charlotte kept a diary during this time. Through her eyes we learn what these years in history were really like. One of the most important days she wrote about in her diary was New Year's Day, 1863. It was Emancipation Day, the day when President Lincoln signed the Emancipation Proclamation. This document set the slaves free all throughout the South.

Charlotte Forten: New Year's Day, Emancipation Day, was a glorious one. We had been invited to visit the camp of the First Regiment of South Carolina Volunteers on that day. It was the greatest day in our nation's history.

The meeting was held in a beautiful live-oak grove near the camp. As I sat on the stand and looked around on the various groups, I thought I had never seen a sight so beautiful. There were the black soldiers, in their blue coats and red pants, the officers in their handsome uniforms, and crowds of men, women, and children under the trees. The faces of all wore a happy, eager, and expectant look.

Sergeant Prince Rivers: As I stood among my fellow soldiers, I couldn't help but remember how a short while ago I had been a slave. Here, on these very islands. But now I was free. And I was willing to die fighting so that every other slave could taste the joys of freedom like I have. I listened to the speeches. What fine ones they were! I was ready to give my speech later on in the day, too.

Soon it was time for the President's Emancipation Proclamation to be read aloud for us all to hear. My heart was moved as I heard those words. Freedom! Oh glorious day! Suddenly, just as the last words of the proclamation were read, my people, all on their own, began to sing.

Group of freedmen—men, women, and children, singing: My country, 'tis of thee,
Sweet land of liberty,
Of thee I sing.
Land where my fathers died,
Land of the pilgrims' pride,
From every mountainside let freedom ring!

Charlotte Forten: After the ceremony, we visited with dear friends who had gathered on this important day. Then there was the Dress Parade—the first I had ever seen. It was a brilliant sight—the long line of men in their brilliant uniforms, with bayonets gleaming in the sunlight. It seemed to me nothing could be more perfect.

After the parade, it was time to go home. We got in our rowboat and headed across the waters to St. Helena's Island. The boatmen sang as they rowed us across.

Boatmen, singing to the tune of "Battle Hymn of the Republic": John Brown's body lies a molding in the grave,
John Brown's body lies a molding in the grave,
John Brown's body lies a molding in the grave,
His soul is marching on!
Glory! Glory! Hallelujah!
Glory! Glory! Glory! Hallelujah!
Glory! Glory! Hallelujah!
His soul is marching on.

Charlotte Forten: Ah, what a grand, glorious day this has been! The dawn of freedom may not break upon us at once. But it will surely come. And sooner, I believe, than we have ever dared hope before. My soul is glad with an exceeding great gladness. "Forever free! Forever free!"—those magical words in the President's Proclamation were constantly singing themselves in my soul.

Narrator: The troops at this important ceremony were the First South Carolina Volunteers. They were the first black regiment of newly freed slaves. Other troops were soon formed. The 54th Massachusetts Volunteers was the first black regiment in the North. They distinguished themselves when they bravely charged

Fort Wagner in Charleston, South Carolina. These African American troops, as well as others, were willing to die so that slavery would never again exist in the nation. Their heroic efforts helped bring victory. In 1865, the Civil War finally came to an end.

Possible Extensions

1. To view a copy of the Emancipation Proclamation, have students visit the following Web site: www.archives.gov/exhibits/featured_documents/emancipation_proclamation/.

    A transcript of the text is available on the Web site: www.archives.gov/exhibits/featured_documents/emancipation_proclamation/transcript.html

2. The Emancipation Proclamation was originally handwritten. Invite students to copy a transcript of the text in their own handwriting. When finished, discuss the meaning of portions of the text and what this document did or did not say about slavery in America.

3. Discuss a current event in American history that your students have witnessed. After the discussion, have students write a diary entry about what they were doing on that significant day.

4. To find out more about what life was like for free African Americans during the Civil War years, invite students to read portions of Charlotte Forten's journal in *A Free Black Girl before the Civil War: The Diary of Charlotte Forten, 1854* (Blue Earth Books, 1998).

5. Have students use the Internet to research Charlotte's famous family of abolitionists, including her grandfather James Forten and her aunt and uncle Robert and Harriet Purvis. Working together on a bulletin board, assemble a family tree of this important family from Philadelphia. (For more information, refer to *A Gentleman of Color: The Life of James Forten* by Julie Winch, Oxford University Press, 2002.)

6. Songs were an important part of freedmen's lives—both while they were enslaved and after they were set free. Using the tune of a familiar patriotic song, write new verses to sing together as a class about the South Carolina Sea Islands, Emancipation Day, and the Civil War.

Politics

United States Senators

Staging

Seat the five Senators in a slight semicircle across the stage so that they are facing the audience. Have the Convention President sit at the side of the stage. In the center front of the stage, place a podium (a desk or music stand may be used instead). When it is each character's turn, that person should walk up to the podium and speak. When finished, he or she should sit down again. If you choose to use props, to represent a political convention make placards from poster board with handles made from paint stirring sticks. Print the Senators' names in large letters on each—one name per placard—and distribute them among the audience so that each student has one to hold. Encourage the audience to show their support of each Senator by holding up their placards.

Characters

Convention President
Audience
Senator Hiram Revels
Senator Blanche Bruce

Senator Edward W. Brooke, III
Senator Carol Moseley Braun
Senator Barack Obama

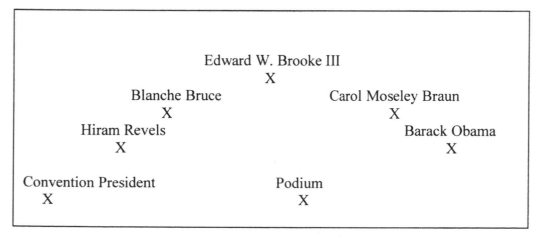

Note: Before performing this play, explain to students that these senators are real people but that most did not live at the same time or even know each other.

Convention President: Welcome to our imaginary political convention! I'd like to introduce our first speaker of the day. Hiram Revels was the very first African American elected to Congress!

Audience: *(Cheers and claps)*

Convention President: A Republican, Senator Revels was elected to the U.S. Senate in 1870, just after the end of the Civil War. Let's give a warm welcome to this Senator from Mississippi!

Audience: *(Cheers and claps)*

Senator Hiram Revels: Thank you! Thank you! As Senator, I was elected by the Mississippi legislature to replace Senator Jefferson Davis. I completed the final year of his term. Jefferson Davis had been president of the Confederate States of America during the Civil War. The Senate needed someone to take his place. I served from 1870 to 1871. It was a short term, but during that time, I used my experiences as a pastor, speaker, and teacher to do the best job I could to represent my state.

I was born free during a time when slavery still existed in our country. I grew up to become a preacher in the A.M.E. Church. I traveled around, even among those who were suffering in slavery, preaching a message of hope. After the Civil War broke out, I helped organize black troops to fight for our country. Education was important to me. I worked to establish schools to teach newly freed slaves.

The years after the Civil War were known as Reconstruction. During those years, I worked with the Freedmen's Bureau to help bring justice to the war-torn South. In 1868, I was elected to the Mississippi State Senate. From there, I was elected to serve in Washington, D.C., as a U.S. Senator. After my term expired, I continued to teach, preach, and lecture. I became president of Alcorn University and devoted the rest of my years to helping my fellow Americans.

Convention President: Thank you, Senator Revels!

Audience: *(Cheers and claps and whistles)*

Convention President: Our next speaker is Blanche Bruce, the very first African American elected to serve a full term as United States Senator!

Audience: *(Cheers and claps)*

Convention President: Also during Reconstruction in Mississippi, Senator Bruce was elected to the U.S. Senate in 1874. Let's give a warm welcome to this Senator!

Audience: *(Cheers and claps)*

Senator Blanche Bruce: Thank you for your generous support! My life is an example that if you set your mind on something, you can do anything. I was born a slave on a plantation in Virginia. Nevertheless, I grew up to become one of the most important political leaders in the nation as a United States Senator.

Education was always important to me. I learned to read and write. At that time, however, it was against the law in most states for slaves to get an education. During the Civil War, I ran away and lived as a fugitive. Finally, the Emancipation Proclamation set me free. One of the first things I did was help open a school for African American students.

After the war, I purchased land. Soon I acquired substantial wealth. I got involved with local politics and began rising up the political ladder. I was elected Sheriff and Superintendent of schools in my state. In 1874 I ran for U.S. Senate—and won! It was an amazing victory and showed the power of the black vote in the South during Reconstruction. During the years I served as Senator, I supported civil rights for all Americans. This included Native Americans, African Americans, and Chinese immigrants to America. I also supported the integration of the armed forces.

After leaving the Senate, I held various political appointments under different presidents. I was appointed twice as the Register of the Treasury and continued an active career in Washington, D.C.

Convention President: Thank you, Senator Bruce!

Audience: *(Cheers and claps and whistles)*

Convention President: Our next speaker is Edward W. Brooke III, the first African American to be elected to the United States Senate in almost 100 years after these first two Senators!

Audience: *(Cheers and claps)*

Convention President: A lawyer by profession, Senator Brooke was elected to the U.S. Senate in 1966. Let's give a warm welcome to this Senator from Massachusetts!

Audience: *(Cheers and claps)*

Senator Edward Brooke: Thank you very much! It's good to be here today and talk about the milestones of my political career. I grew up in Washington, D.C. My father was a lawyer. I knew how important politics could be.

I was drafted into the U.S. Army during World War II. In the army, I used my knowledge of law to defend other enlisted men in court. I was part of the all-black 366th Regiment. We were shipped overseas to Italy. Among other duties, I disguised myself as an Italian and crossed over enemy lines. I received the bronze star for my heroism in action. After the war was over, I earned my law degree at Boston University. My law practice flourished. I also started getting involved in local politics in Massachusetts. My voice could be heard fighting crime and political corruption. I held various government positions including being sworn in as Attorney General. In 1967 I was elected to the U.S.

Senate. I was the first African American Senator since the years just after the Civil War.

During the two terms I served as U.S. Senator, I used my powerful position to continue the fight against crime and corruption. I was the first Republican Senator to challenge Nixon to resign because of his political scandal as President of the United States. I also supported civil rights. I fought successfully to pass the 1968 Civil Rights Act. After leaving the Senate, I continued with my career in law. Throughout my lifetime, I was awarded more than thirty honorary degrees. I also received many honors and awards, including the prestigious Springharn Medal from the NAACP.

Convention President: Thank you, Senator Brooke!

Audience: *(Cheers and claps and whistles)*

Convention President: Our next speaker is Carol Moseley Braun, the first African American woman elected as a United States Senator!

Audience: *(Cheers and claps)*

Convention President: Also a lawyer, Senator Moseley Braun was elected to the U.S. Senate in 1992. Let's give a warm welcome to this Senator from Illinois!

Audience: *(Cheers and claps)*

Senator Carol Moseley Braun: Thank you for your support! It's exciting to be known as someone who accomplished many firsts. This was in the political arena both as a woman and as an African American.

Growing up in Chicago's South Side, I attended the University of Illinois at Chicago. I became a lawyer. Before long, I was involved with politics. In 1978 I was elected to the Illinois House of Representatives. People knew me as a champion for getting things done. My special field of interest was education. I sponsored many bills to improve educational conditions in Chicago. I also supported bills to end discrimination in situations such as buying a new house.

As part of the Illinois state legislature, I became the first woman to be an assistant majority leader of the House. I was also the first African American to hold this position. Eventually, I became the recorder of deeds in Cook County. I was the first woman and African American to hold an executive position there.

In 1992, I was elected to the U.S. Senate. I was the first African American woman to be a U.S. Senator. I was also the fourth African American U.S. Senator in our history. Once there, I again sponsored bills to improve education.

After I left the Senate, President Bill Clinton appointed me as an ambassador to New Zealand. It was a tropical paradise! When that position came to an end, I decided to run a short time as a candidate for the presidential elections of 2004. Since then I have returned to practicing law in Chicago.

Convention President: Thank you, Senator Moseley Braun!

Audience: *(Cheers and claps and whistles)*

Convention President: Our next speaker is Barack Obama, the fifth African American to be elected to the United States Senate.

Audience: *(Cheers and claps)*

Convention President: Drawing as big of a crowd as a rock star, Senator Obama was elected to the U.S. Senate in 2004. Let's give a warm welcome to this Senator from Illinois!

Audience: *(Cheers and claps)*

Senator Barack Obama: Here in America—the land of the free—anyone can rise up to become a political leader. My father was from Kenya, Africa. He grew up in a small village there, herding goats. Eager to get a good education, he was eventually selected to attend the University of Hawaii. It was half way around the world. There he met my mother, a young woman from Kansas. She was also attending the University of Hawaii. They married, and I was born in Honolulu.

I was still very young when my father left the family. My mother remarried. We moved to Indonesia with my new stepfather. After several years there, my mother sent me to live with my grandparents back in Hawaii. She hoped I would get a good education there.

Eventually, I went to New York City where I graduated from Columbia University. After graduation, I took a job in the South Side of Chicago. During that time, I decided to become a lawyer. After graduating from Harvard Law School, I returned to Chicago. Once there, I practiced civil rights law. It was my job to defend people in court who were fighting for their civil rights.

In 1996, my political career was launched when I was elected to the Illinois state Senate. I was invited to speak at the 2004 Democratic convention. With that famous speech, it was as if I became a star. That same year, I was elected to the United States Senate. And for the 2008 presidential elections, I announced that I was running for President.

With my book, *Audacity of Hope,* I became known for my new politics. I offered hope to every American, rich and poor, black and white, man and woman. Together we can bridge the gaps between our differences. Together, we can work through the problems we face in our country. Together, we can build a better America!

Convention President: Thank you, Senator Obama!

Audience: (*Cheers and claps and whistles*)

Convention President: That wraps up our speeches for the day. Thank you for coming! And remember—your vote is what makes these success stories happen. Vote—and make a difference in America. Vote—and make a difference in our world!

Possible Extensions

1. To help students understand what a political convention is really like, show them excerpts from videos found online. If possible, search the Internet to find a video clip of Barack Obama's Keynote Address at the 2004 Democratic Convention.

2. Make a timeline with your students to show national and world events that were taking place during the years each of these five Senators served. Include current events for the most recent Senators. For more details and dates, refer to the following books:

   The Timetables of African American History by Sharon Harley (New York: Simon & Schuster, 1995).

   The Timetables of History by Bernard Grun (New York: Simon & Schuster, 2005).

3. Have students create their own time capsules about current events in America and the world today. Place tiny items of interest, photographs, campaign buttons, or small pictures in two clear plastic cups with their open ends taped together to form a container. Have students take these time capsules home and save them until the *next* African American is elected to the U.S. Senate. At that time, they can open up their time capsules and see how things have changed since they studied about the first five African American Senators.

4. Nearly 100 years passed from the time the first two Senators were elected until the third African American Senator was voted into office. Discuss various events and situations that occurred in America from 1865 to 1965 and how these affected our country's political arena such as educational opportunities for African Americans, Jim Crow laws, voter restriction practices, availability of media, and accessibility of the TV or Internet.

5. Invite students to imagine they are speech writers for Senator Barack Obama. Have them each write an inspirational speech about hope for all Americans to work together to bridge differences between the various races, cultures, wealth, and opinions throughout our nation. Allow time to share speeches with the class.

6. Barack Obama wrote an autobiography about his childhood. Encourage students to write an autobiography of the highlights of their own childhood. Use report folders to assemble these into small "books" with a picture of the author on the cover. Display the books and encourage students to read them during spare time.

7. Make a bulletin board of inspirational quotes from Barack Obama. Have students look through his autobiographies or choose one of his many quotes featured in the book *Hopes and Dreams: The Story of Barack Obama* by Steve Dougherty (Black Dog & Leventhal Publishers, 2007). Give each student a piece of white construction paper to cut out a shape of a large speech bubble. Have them each choose one quote that inspires them the most and write it on the speech bubble. Display these speech bubbles on the bulletin board with a picture of Obama. Add the title, *Barack Obama Says …*

Tuskegee Airmen

True American Heroes

Staging

Position the narrator at the front side of the stage. General Benjamin O. Davis, Jr. may sit on a stool at the center of the stage. Two reporters can stand, one on each side of him, throughout the interview.

Characters

Narrator   Reporters 1 and 2
General Davis

General Benjamin O. Davis, Jr.
X

Reporter   Reporter
X   X

Narrator
X

May be copied for classroom use. From *Readers Theatre for African American History* by Jeff Sanders and Nancy Sanders. Westport, CT:

57

Narrator: On July 26, 1948, President Harry S Truman announced Executive Order 9981. It brought an end to the years of racism and segregation in the military. From that day on, the order stated, the armed forces would become a place for equal opportunity and equal treatment of all races. It was a historic event.

Before that time, most doors in the military were closed to African Americans. During World War II, however, the U.S. Army Air Force trained an all-black unit of pilots to fly during the war. These pilots became known as the Tuskegee Airmen.

Here with us today is the chief commanding officer of the Tuskegee Airmen, General Benjamin O. Davis, Jr. In this fictionalized scene, General Davis is being interviewed by two reporters.

Reporter 1: General Davis, many folks have heard of the famous Tuskegee Airmen. But few really know their story. Who exactly were the Tuskegee Airmen? And how did they earn their fame?

General Davis: It's a long story. One that is filled with both tragedy and triumph. Where would you like me to begin?

Reporter 2: Could you tell us a little bit about yourself first? Your family history? Your background?

General Davis: Certainly. My father is Benjamin O. Davis, Sr. He was a military man himself, and rose up through the ranks to become the first African American general in the United States Army. He encouraged me to apply to West Point and go there for officer training.

Reporter 1: What was it like for you as a cadet in West Point?

General Davis: It was one of the most difficult things I ever did. Racism and prejudice were so bad at West Point that they put me through their silencing treatment. For four long years, not a single other cadet spoke to me. They made me sit alone on the bus, eat by myself, and do everything by myself. No one would even be my roommate. They tried to make it so bad they hoped I would quit. But with each terrible injustice I suffered, I determined to work even harder. I knew it was up to me to stick through it, tough times and all. My goal was always to do my best so I could open doors for other African Americans in the military and help bring segregation and racism to an end.

Reporter 2: Your hard work paid off. You graduated 35th in a class of 276. Congratulations!

General Davis: Thank you.

Reporter 1: By that time, the world was at war. America hadn't yet joined the fight, but President F. D. Roosevelt started to build up our armed forces. Congress passed a law to allow universities to begin training airplane pilots for the army. How did that affect you?

General Davis: Tuskegee Institute in Alabama was appointed as the site to train the nation's first unit of all-black pilots. Along with twelve cadets, I came to the Tuskegee Army Air Field. I was the officer in training. On March 7, 1942, four of those cadets and I earned our wings. I became captain of the 99th Pursuit Squadron.

One day, First Lady Eleanor Roosevelt visited Tuskegee. Against the wishes of her Secret Service men, she asked to take an airplane ride with our flight instructor, Charles A. "Chief" Anderson. She used the photograph of that famous event to show her support of African Americans in the military.

Reporter 2: America had been in the war since Japan bombed Pearl Harbor on December 7, 1941. How soon did the 99th Pursuit Squadron join the fight?

General Davis: On April 15, 1943, the 99th Pursuit Squadron shipped out to northern Africa. We had a full support crew along with us. Technicians and medics came, too. We began to see action and flew on missions near Sicily and Italy.

Reporter 1: Reports were that you experienced racism overseas as well.

General Davis: Yes. Some white Army Air Force officers were prejudiced and didn't like having black pilots fighting in the war. They tried to get new orders to send us back to America. I fought to keep the Tuskegee Airmen active overseas, however. I went back to Washington, D.C., and spoke to the War Department. I gave them examples of our outstanding service. It worked! We were not forced to return home.

Reporter 2: By this time, the Air Force was having troubles. They were losing a lot of bombers to enemy planes. It was a huge loss to our forces. But you did something about it, didn't you?

General Davis: I knew the military could count on the Tuskegee Airmen. Our pilots were some of the finest in the world. I knew these men. They were brave and dedicated to serving our country, even though our country still did not treat us as equals. As commander of the new 332nd Fighter Group, I knew we could help protect the bombers from enemy planes.

Reporter 1: Wasn't the 332nd Fighter Group known as the famous "Red Tails"?

General Davis: That's right. We flew P-51 Mustangs. These were fast little planes. The reason we were called the Red Tails is because we painted the tails of these planes a bright red. Everyone knew the Tuskegee Airmen were flying when they saw our planes.

Reporter 2: How did the Red Tails protect the bombers?

General Davis: We flew on escort missions. This means that we flew right beside the bombers to protect them as they headed over enemy territory. When we saw enemy planes, we shot them down before they could shoot our bombers. The Red Tails flew on 200 bomber escort missions and we never lost a single bomber.

Reporter 1: That's an amazing record! Of all your missions, was there one that stands out from the rest?

General Davis: Plans were put into action for bombers to target one of the most important cities in Germany—Berlin. On March 24, 1945 I led 54 pilots as escorts for these bombers. It was an extremely dangerous assignment. It was one of the longest runs in the history of the Air Force. But we did it. We flew all the way round trip from Italy to Berlin and kept our record intact. Not a single bomber was shot down.

Reporter 2: You never lost a bomber, but did you ever lose any of your men?

General Davis: The fighting was fierce at times, but our planes always stayed with the bombers to protect them from enemy fire. As a result, sixty-six of our men were killed in action.

Reporter 1: To honor the brave actions of these American heroes, the Tuskegee Airmen received many distinguished awards. Among other honors, you earned the Distinguished Flying Cross.

General Davis: What a meaningful day that was! My father attended the ceremony and pinned the medal on my shirt. I knew he was proud of me. He was proud of all the Tuskegee Airmen.

Reporter 2: Finally, World War II came to an end. What happened to the Tuskegee Airmen after the war?

General Davis: The Tuskegee Airmen returned home to America with the rest of the military. When President Truman issued Executive Order 9981, it brought an end to segregation in the armed forces and an end to the Tuskegee Airmen. These men either retired from active duty or were integrated into the rest of the military.

Narrator: The Tuskegee Airmen will never be forgotten. The 332nd won more than 100 Distinguished Flying Crosses and three Distinguished Unit Citations. In 1998, Benjamin O. Davis, Jr. became a four-star general. President Bill Clinton had the honor of pinning the fourth star on his shoulder. In 2007, 200 Tuskegee Airmen were invited to a special ceremony at the White House where they received the Congressional Gold Medal. These brave men are remembered as true American heroes.

Possible Extensions

1. The Tuskegee Airmen won many distinguished awards for their hard work, patriotism, and bravery. To read about General Davis, Jr.'s outstanding military career and view some of the medals he received, visit the Web site: www.arlingtoncemetery. net/bodavisjr.htm. Ask students to draw pictures of an original medal design. When finished, take a class vote to choose a medal to use as a reward for hard work and outstanding classroom behavior. Photocopy the medal and award it to deserving students throughout the year.

2. Have students write a list of questions they would like to ask General Davis, Jr. about what it was like as a cadet at West Point, as an officer-in-training at Tuskegee, and as commander of the famous Red Tails. Invite several volunteers to take turns acting as General Davis, Jr. Let students ask their questions to General Davis, Jr., pretending to be reporters. Encourage the actors to answer what they think the general might actually say.

3. The 332nd decorated their planes by painting the tails a bright red color. This came to be known as a symbol of their bravery and amazing ability as pilots. Provide paper for students to draw an airplane and decorate it with stripes or bright colors for their own imaginary flight squadron. When finished, ask them to share what the designs and colors represent.

   Show students a picture of a P-51 Mustang or "Red Tail." See the Web site: www.nasm.si.edu/blackwings/hdetail/detailbw.cfm?bwID=BW0071.

4. To view a collection of photographs of the Tuskegee Airmen, visit the Prints and Photographs Division of the Library of Congress at the following Web site: http://www. loc.gov/rr/print/. Click on the link to the online catalog. Click to search inside the catalog. Then search for "332nd" in the search field.

5. World War II affected people all over the world. Encourage students to interview family members and discover what their own relatives were doing during the war. Allow time for students to share photographs and stories of relatives involved with the war.

The Great Migration

Moving North to a Better Life

Staging

The two narrators can stand together at the side of the stage. The remaining characters in each scene should all stand as a group in the center of the stage as they talk with each other. If they are not in a scene, the characters can wait offstage. During Scene 3, the stage can be set up like a small classroom, with several rows of students sitting in chairs.

Characters

Narrators 1 and 2   Joseph
Daisy   Uncle Henry
Julia   Mrs. Bentley
Mrs. Cooper   Teacher
Mr. Cooper   Class

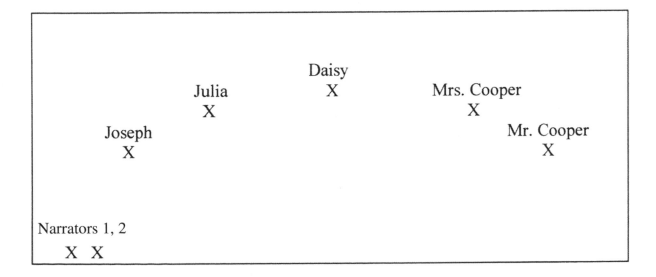

Scene 1

Setting: Train ride from Atlanta, Georgia, to Washington, D.C.

Narrator 1: When America fought in World War I, its doors became closed to European immigrants. Up to that time, many factories in northern cities were filled with workers who had moved to America from countries in Europe. Now there were no new workers arriving from across the Atlantic. More workers were needed than ever before, however. Northern factories were busy making war supplies.

Narrator 2: Where could these factories find workers to build everything they needed? The South! Soon, labor recruiters traveled to southern states looking for workers. They offered better jobs, better education, and a better life. Many African Americans living in the South decided to move North. Entire families packed their bags and moved. So many people moved North that this became known as the "Great Migration."

Narrator 1: Today we see a fictitious family who used to live on a farm near Atlanta, Georgia. They are traveling north on a train to Washington, D.C.

Narrator 2: Their uncle wrote them a letter telling them to come. Everything they own is stuffed inside the suitcases they carry. It's been a long, hot trip.

Daisy: Ma, how much longer do we have to ride this train? It's so dirty and smelly and hot.

Julia: It's so noisy I can't sleep.

Mrs. Cooper: I know. You've both been such a big help already watching your little brother. It won't be much longer.

Mr. Cooper: We should reach Washington, D.C., any time now. It's our next stop.

Joseph: Where are we going to sleep? I'm tired of this old train.

Mrs. Cooper: We'll stay with Uncle Henry. He sent us a letter telling us to come. His place is just a one room apartment, but he said we could share his rent until we found a place of our own.

Mr. Cooper: He said I'd find factory work right away. And there's a school. You girls will finally get the education you deserve.

Mrs. Cooper: The school is called the National Training School for Women and Girls. Nannie Helen Burroughs is the president.

Joseph: I remember when she came to visit our church and spoke.

Julia: I've never heard someone speak such fine words as she did.

Daisy: Doesn't she go to Uncle Henry's church, too?

Mrs. Cooper: Yes. The Nineteenth Street Baptist. It's in Washington, D.C. Uncle Henry said it's a wonderful church.

Mr. Cooper: Uncle Henry said folks at the church will help us get settled into life in the big city. It might be hard, but they'll help us make the change. After our struggle on the farm, it will be a welcome change.

Narrator 1: Finally, the train stopped at the station.

Narrator 2: Everyone picked up their suitcases and got off the train.

Mr. Cooper: Henry! Over here!

Uncle Henry: My, oh my! You all are a sight to make a man smile.

Joseph: Uncle Henry! We rode on the train all the way to see you.

Uncle Henry: And look how you've grown. You're a foot taller than when I last laid eyes on you.

Mrs. Cooper: We don't want to put you out now, Henry. With our whole family settling into your apartment and all. We'll find a place of our own soon enough.

Daisy: We'll help cook.

Julia: We'll help when we're not busy at school.

Mr. Cooper: Now, now, girls. There will be plenty of time for all that talk later. First I have to find myself a job.

Narrator 1: The Coopers followed Uncle Henry down the streets of the city. They finally came to his apartment and took their things inside. It was crowded, but it felt good to be off the train and have a roof over their heads.

Scene 2

Setting: Small apartment in Washington, D.C.

Narrator 2: After a good night's sleep, everyone woke up bright and early. The sounds of the city were all around them.

Mr. Cooper: Uncle Henry's going to introduce me to his boss at the factory today.

Uncle Henry: He'll be sure to get hired right away. They always need more workers. We'll be home tonight and tell you all the news.

Mr. Cooper: Good-bye!

Mrs. Cooper and the children: Good-bye!

Narrator 1: Mr. Cooper and Uncle Henry left for work. Later in the morning, there was a knock at the door.

Mrs. Bentley: Good morning!

Mrs. Cooper: Good morning.

Mrs. Bentley: Folks at the church told me that Henry had family moving in with him. I'm from the National Urban League. It's our job to help folks like you settle into your new life here in the city.

Mrs. Cooper: That's a mighty kind thing for you to do.

Mrs. Bentley: There are so many thousands of people moving here, and so many folks needing help, that we make it our goal to help them. We help them find a home, get enrolled in school, and find jobs.

Mrs. Cooper: I'm thinking I need to find work to do. Back home in Georgia I used to take in washing and do wealthy people's laundry.

Joseph: Ma boiled the clothes in a big pot in our yard.

Mrs. Cooper: I could do laundry here, too, but there's no place to boil the water. This apartment is too small. And outside there isn't any yard. Only the busy street.

Mrs. Bentley: I know several people who are looking for someone to do their laundry. You will have to go to their houses and do the work, though. Life is different here in the city.

Julia: How can Ma do that? Joseph is too little to be left alone.

Daisy: Julia and I can't watch him. We're planning on going to school.

Mrs. Bentley: I know a woman named Mrs. Tanner. She takes in other children whose mothers have to work. She'll watch Joseph any time you need her.

Narrator 2: Mrs. Bentley gave all the information to Mrs. Cooper that she needed to know. After she left, the girls both talked at once.

Daisy: Does this mean we can start school tomorrow?

Julia: Yes, can we?

Mrs. Cooper: We'll get our things unpacked here today. If your father gets a job, then I'll go to work tomorrow, too. You can go to school.

Narrator 1: The girls helped their mother unpack and settle in. It was crowded, but they hoped they would soon make enough money to have an apartment of their own.

Narrator 2: Late that night, Uncle Henry and Mr. Cooper came home.

Joseph: Pa's home!

Daisy: How was your first day in the city, Pa?

Julia: Did you get a job?

Uncle Henry: My boss hired him right away. It was just like I told you it would be.

Mr. Cooper: Yes. We'll have food on our table once again.

Mrs. Cooper: What was your day like?

Mr. Cooper: City life is surely different than country life. A factory is like a giant machine. It has time clocks and assembly lines. It's a busy place.

Mrs. Cooper: But we'll not be working out in the hot sun all day. And the girls won't have to pick cotton anymore. They're starting school tomorrow! Soon we'll get a place of our own. I found work, too. A woman from the National Urban League stopped by and helped us out.

Scene 3

Setting: The National Training School for Women and Girls

Narrator 1: The next day, Daisy and Julia enrolled in the National Training School for Women and Girls. They were excited to start their first day of school.

Teacher: Good morning, class. Today we have two new students.

Class: Good morning.

Teacher: The founder and president of our school, Miss Nannie Helen Burroughs, calls this the school of three B's. Who knows what that stands for?

Class: Bible, bath, and broom.

Teacher: Very good! Miss Burroughs believes that a clean life, a clean body, and a clean house are good qualities for every young woman to have. And what is our motto?

Class: "We Specialize in the Wholly Impossible."

Teacher: Excellent. By working hard and getting a good education, we can take pride in who we are. We can live a better life.

Narrator 2: On their first day at school, Daisy and Julia joined the other young women in their classes. That night when they returned to Uncle Henry's apartment, they had a lot to talk about.

Scene 4

Setting: Uncle Henry's apartment

Daisy: We get to learn bookkeeping and how to be a store clerk!

Mrs. Cooper: Well! That is fancy learning indeed! But what about learning practical skills?

Julia: We have classes where we'll learn how to be housekeepers and maids, too.

Daisy: They'll teach us how to do laundry and cook and sew. We're learning how to do everything.

Julia: Even how to read the Bible.

Mr. Cooper: New jobs, new home, and new schools. New freedom and new hope. It's a new life here in the city and it's hard, but we'll make it through.

Narrator 1: In the early 1900s and on up through the 1940s, thousands of African Americans left the South and moved North in the Great Migration.

Narrator 2: After the Civil War, the South had become an unbearable place to stay for many African Americans. Segregation laws took away their rights. Lynchings, mob violence, and the Ku Klux Klan brought terror into their lives. They could not make enough money as farmers to earn a decent living.

Narrator 1: Thousands moved to find jobs in factories up North such as in Pittsburgh's steel mills, Detroit's auto industry, and Chicago's meat packinghouses.

Narrator 2: Organizations and schools were started to help meet the needs of the masses of newcomers. Together, they worked to build a better life.

Possible Extensions

1. Make a timeline with your students from 1910 through 1940 to show national and world events that were taking place during the Great Migration. For more details and dates, refer to the following books:

   The Timetables of African American History by Sharon Harley (New York: Simon & Schuster, 1995).

   The Timetables of History by Bernard Grun (New York: Simon & Schuster, 1991).

2. Divide students into four groups. Assign each group one city to research: Chicago, Detroit, Pittsburgh, and Washington, D.C. Have students look up the history of that city, its natural resources, its main industries, and how it was affected during the Great Migration. Allow time for each group to share their research with the class. Discuss how life could have been different for various families depending on which city they moved to during this era.

3. Many organizations were started in various cities to help newcomers adjust to their different surroundings. Ask students to share what they remember about their first day of school. Think of a way to help newcomers transition to your school such as with Playground Pals or a Homework Club. Have your class start an organization to help new students who arrive.

4. The National Training School for Women and Girls taught its students practical living skills as well as job skills. This helped train young women how to get employment as well as improve living conditions in their own home. Turn your classroom into a Training-School-For-A-Day. To prepare, divide students into six or more stations, with four students at each station. Assign half of the stations each a different life skill such as learning how to do laundry, balancing a checkbook, or sewing on a button. Assign the other half of the stations each a different job skill such as writing a letter on the computer, selling products in a store, or working in a restaurant. Help students set up a demonstration at each station. When the stations are ready, invite two students from each station to take turns visiting all the other stations. Then switch places and let the remaining students visit the stations.

5. The National Training School for Women and Girls was known as the school of three B's. Pick a theme for your classroom or school. Invite students to make posters and decorate your door to support this theme and inspire everyone to do his or her best.

Harlem Renaissance

Zora Neale Hurston and the Rent Party

Staging

The three narrators can sit on stools at the side of the stage. The remaining characters in each scene should stand as a group in the center of the stage. In the second scene, a chair and desk can be used to represent the piano. Characters not yet in a scene can wait offstage. Scene 1 opens with Zora Neale Hurston and Langston Hughes standing in the center of the stage.

Characters

Narrators 1, 2, and 3   Selma Burke
Langston Hughes   Paul Robeson
Zora Neale Hurston   Duke Ellington
Wayside Printer   James VanDerZee

```
            Zora Neale Hurston   Langston Hughes
                    X                   X




Narrators
X X X
```

Narrator 1: During the Great Migration, many African Americans moved to Harlem, a section of New York City. So many artists, writers, and performers flocked to this part of the country during the 1920s and 1930s that it became known as the Harlem Renaissance. Plays, poetry, jazz, culture, and scholarly achievement could be seen and heard everywhere. Pride in African roots grew strong.

Narrator 2: Many people moved to Harlem to escape a life of poverty in the South. They soon discovered conditions weren't much better in the busy, noisy city. Apartments were crowded. Rent was high, and wages were low. But hope was strong. A new kind of social event developed, one that was based on the tradition of church socials and fundraisers in the South. It was called a rent party. People paid for a ticket to get in and also paid to buy plates of food. Harlem rent parties became very popular during these years, and the hosts collected enough money to pay their rent.

Narrator 3: Let's visit a street in Harlem where a fictitious rent party is about to take place. Each of the characters at the party were actual artists and performers who knew each other during the Harlem Renaissance, but they might not have all gone to the same rent party at the same time. Let's see what takes place.

Scene 1

Setting: Street in Harlem, a section of New York City

Langston Hughes: Good morning, Zora! What are you doing out this early?

Zora Neale Hurston: I'm getting ready for a rent party. You know my rent is due on Monday. If I don't give the money to the landlord, he'll put all my furniture out here on the street on Tuesday.

Langston Hughes: A rent party sounds like fun. Who is going to play?

Zora Neale Hurston: Duke Ellington is playing at the Cotton Club Saturday night. First we can dance to his music while we listen to him on the radio. After he's done there, he promised to come by my place and play the piano for us.

Langston Hughes: That will keep everyone's toes tapping. The Duke's got the best sound around.

Narrator 1: Just then a Wayside Printer man walked up the street pushing his cartload of printing tools.

Wayside Printer: Get your cards and get them fast! Print them while you wait!

Zora Neale Hurston: Hey there! Can you print up some small cards for my rent party?

Wayside Printer: Of course! What do you want the cards to say?

Zora Neale Hurston: Let's call it a Tea Party. Put my address on there and tell everyone to come on Saturday.

Langston Hughes: Put a nice jingle on there, too. How about, "The Duke's got the sound. So how about coming around? Listen to the piano man and come dance to his famous band."

Zora Neale Hurston: That will bring people in.

Wayside Printer: *(Handing Zora a stack of small cards.)* Here you are. Will this be enough?

Zora Neale Hurston: That's plenty! I'll put them all around town.

Langston Hughes: Here, let me have some, too. I'll give them out to our friends. See you Saturday!

Scene 2

Setting: Zora's apartment in Harlem on Saturday night

Zora Neale Hurston: Help me move this furniture out of the way, Selma. I want to clear out the whole room so we have plenty of space to dance.

Selma Burke: Let's put everything in the back rooms of the apartment. Keep the kitchen clear, though. Neighbors are already starting to bring in the food.

Zora Neale Hurston: Let's put the piano next to the window. That way everyone will know that the Duke's here tonight. We'll have a huge crowd! I'll collect enough money to pay the rent for sure.

Selma Burke: I brought my favorite recipe of fried chicken. I saw pickled pig's feet and potato salad in the kitchen, too.

Zora Neale Hurston: It sure smells good!

Narrator 2: Just then they heard a knock at the door.

Paul Robeson: Has the party started yet, Zora? Here's my quarter to come in.

Zora Neale Hurston: You're the first to come! I didn't expect to see you, though. Aren't you performing tonight at the theater?

Paul Robeson: Opening night for *The Emperor Jones* isn't until next Saturday. I'll get you a ticket so you can be sure to come.

Zora Neale Hurston: That's great! I love watching you act. And listening to you sing. Do you think you might want to entertain us with your fine bass voice tonight?

Paul Robeson: Will the Duke be here?

Selma Burke: He's coming by after his show is over at the Cotton Club.

Paul Robeson: I'll get him to play some spirituals and sing to that. You know I'm getting ready to give a concert. I plan to only sing spirituals for the entire show.

Zora Neale Hurston: I heard. With my background as an anthropologist and my love of folktales, I'm glad you're performing spirituals. Those are songs we can be proud of.

Narrator 3: More knocks sounded at the door. And more. Soon the house was filled and the radio was blaring. Neighbors and friends danced in the crowded room to the music on the radio of Duke Ellington and his orchestra playing live at the Cotton Club. Then the music stopped. Guests went into the kitchen where they bought plates of delicious home-cooked food. Soon there was another knock at the door.

Zora Neale Hurston: Duke Ellington's here, everyone! Hi, Duke!

Duke Ellington: Hi, Zora. Sorry I couldn't be here earlier.

Zora Neale Hurston: That's all right. We tuned in to listen to your band on the radio until you could come. All our friends are here. Paul Robeson, Selma, and Langston. And James VanDerZee's here with his camera.

James VanDerZee: How about if you sit down at the piano, Duke? Let's have everyone gather around you at the keyboard. I'll take a picture of the party.

Selma Burke: Come on, everyone! Gather around.

James VanDerZee: Duke, sit at the bench and put your hands on the piano keys. Paul, stand next to the piano and look like you're singing a spiritual.

Paul Robeson: How does this look?

James VanDerZee: Great! Now Langston, Zora, and Selma, lean on the piano like you're listening to Duke play. Everyone else can crowd in close around you.

Langston Hughes: Hurry up and get in place for the picture everyone! Then the real party will start when Duke starts to play.

Narrator 1: Soon everyone crowded around the piano and the photograph was taken. Then Duke began to play and the crowd danced the night away. After a while Langston Hughes stood by the piano and watched Duke's fingers fly across the keys.

Langston Hughes: That's fine playing on the piano tonight, Duke.

Duke Ellington: Thanks! Even though I'm famous for leading my orchestra, playing the piano is still my favorite thing to do.

Langston Hughes: Are you working on anything new?

Duke Ellington: Always am. Billy Strayhorn is working on a new song for me called "Take the 'A' Train." You've never heard anything like it. It's going to be big. But how about you? Are you working on anything new yourself?

Langston Hughes: Oh, you know me. Always writing a new poem, an article, or a novel. In fact Zora and I are working on a new play together called *Mule Bone*.

Duke Ellington: Is that so? It should be good. Anything you put your hand to usually is.

Narrator 2: The rent party lasted until dawn. Plenty of money was collected to pay the rent. Good food and good times were enjoyed by all.

Narrator 3: It was quite a crowd that gathered at our imaginary rent party. Zora Neale Hurston was a famous author and anthropologist. She collected African American folklore and published it in her writings. Langston Hughes became known as the poet laureate of Harlem. In his poems and other writings, he expressed what it was like to be an African American living during the Harlem Renaissance.

Narrator 1: Selma Burke was a sculptor who created many sculptures of well-known African American men and women. She became famous for her bronze plaque of President Franklin D. Roosevelt. It was used as the basis for his portrait on the dime. Duke Ellington is considered by many to be the most important jazz songwriter.

Narrator 2: A star athlete, Paul Robeson went on to become a world famous singer and actor. He performed on Broadway and in London and will always be remembered for his starring role in *Othello*. James VanDerZee captured the Harlem Renaissance in pictures. He took photographs of political leaders, celebrities, and sports teams as well as everyday life in Harlem.

Narrator 3: Together these artists, writers, scholars, and performers changed America. Together, with many others who shared the same visions and the same dreams, they changed the world.

Possible Extensions

1. Host a Harlem Rent Party! Invite guests to dress in the '20s styles. Serve southern-style foods. Dance to recordings of Duke Ellington and his orchestra. Donate proceeds from ticket and food sales to a local homeless shelter.

2. Read favorite poems of Langston Hughes aloud with your students. Listen to the author read one of his most famous poems, "The Negro Speaks of Rivers," by visiting the following Web site: www.poets.org/viewmedia.php/prmMID/1722.

3. Zora Neale Hurston collected folklore and published it in her writings. Create a student folklore collection and "publish" it in a class book. Ask students to write original versions of favorite childhood stories they heard when they were young. Assemble these pages together in a book to share as a class.

4. James VanDerZee took photos of everyday life in Harlem. Discuss why his collection of photographs has historic value today. Decorate a bulletin board with photographs you and your students bring in depicting everyday life in your homes, school, and community. When the bulletin board is completed, discuss why these photos have historic value even though they portray ordinary people, places, and things.

5. Paul Robeson became famous for his role in Shakespeare's *Othello*. Choose one of Shakespeare's plays (or portions of one) to have your students read aloud and perform as a readers theatre script.

The Great Debate

Booker T. Washington and W.E.B. Du Bois Lead the Way

Staging

Have three podiums on the stage (music stands or desks may be used instead). The two moderators should stand at the center podium. The three members of Team A should stand together at the podium on the left of the stage. The three members of Team B should stand together at the podium on the right of the stage.

Characters

Moderators 1 and 2   Team A: Members 1, 2, and 3
Team B: Members 1, 2, and 3

Team A	Moderators	Team B
X	X	X

Note: At the end of the script, each member on the debate teams has "blanks" included for part of their script. These are for the students to complete, either as part of a pre-performance writing assignment, or during the play itself.

Moderator 1: Today our debate teams will discuss one of the biggest debates of all time. Different opinions were held by two African American leaders in the years after the Civil War. Their disagreement became so strong that it became known as the Great Debate. What did they disagree about? Their debate was about how African Americans should change from living as slaves to living as free citizens in America.

Moderator 2: Team A is here with us to represent the side who supported Booker T. Washington. He was the famous educator who founded Tuskegee Institute in Alabama. Team B is here to represent the side who supported W.E.B. Du Bois. He was the great scholar and writer who was the editor of the Nation Association for the Advancement of Colored People's (NAACP) magazine, *The Crisis*. Let's listen to what they have to say about the Great Debate.

Moderator 1: First of all, I would like you to comment on how conditions were for African Americans during the late 1800s to early 1900s. These were the years just after the end of the Civil War. Team A, would you please comment first?

Team A: Supporters of Booker T. Washington

Member 1: When Booker T. Washington arrived in Alabama in 1881, he found a South still suffering after losing the Civil War. Many people, both black and white, were very, very poor. It was a struggle just to grow enough food to eat and make enough clothes to wear.

Team A: Supporters of Booker T. Washington

Member 2: There was still a lot of anger from local whites, many of whom used to own slaves. Booker T. Washington knew about this difficulty. He tried to get the local whites to accept the school he planned to build. He wanted to convince them that a school was necessary to train African Americans how to become better workers so they could help rebuild a strong South. He explained his plans to teach former slaves how to work with their hands to become better farmers, cooks, housecleaners, and teachers.

Team A: Supporters of Booker T. Washington

Member 3: Washington opened the doors to his new school on July 4, 1881. The African American students he taught were very, very poor. He was their only teacher. His supplies were few. He hardly had any money to finish building the school. He felt he would need the support of wealthy whites to donate money to help the school survive.

Moderator 2: Team B, would you like to comment about what life was like for African Americans after the Civil War?

Team B: Supporters of W.E.B. Du Bois

Member 1: W.E.B. Du Bois grew up in Massachusetts. He attended college at Fisk University in Nashville, Tennessee. When he arrived at Fisk, it was the first time he had ever been in the South. His new friends and fellow classmates told him about the racism and segregation that was there. Even though slavery no longer existed, many whites still treated blacks as if they were slaves.

Team B: Supporters of W.E.B. Du Bois

Member 2: During the summer, W.E.B. Du Bois taught school to African American children living in rural Tennessee. He saw how poor everyone was. He heard spirituals being sung about what life was like when there had been slavery. He taught in rundown schoolhouses without any supplies, but everywhere he went, he found African Americans hungry to learn.

Team B: Supporters of W.E.B. Du Bois

Member 3: Du Bois disagreed with Booker T. Washington's opinion that the best way for newly freed slaves to succeed was mainly to teach them to work with their hands. W.E.B. Du

Bois felt that schools should offer strong academics to inspire young African Americans to reach for the stars. He felt that everyone should have the right to a great education, no matter what color their skin was or where they were from. He didn't think they should just take classes on how to become better cooks or farmers.

Moderator 1: All across America, people heard about the Great Debate. Everyone had a strong opinion. Some supported Washington. Others supported Du Bois. Team A, would you please comment about why people supported Booker T. Washington?

Team A: Supporters of Booker T. Washington

Member 1: There was a violent struggle going on in American politics after the Civil War. Throughout the South, whites tried to keep blacks from being voted into government office. Jim Crow, or racist, laws were passed to stop African Americans from voting and to keep blacks segregated, or apart, from whites. It was a terrible time, and a lot of African Americans were killed.

Team A: Supporters of Booker T. Washington

Member 2: Booker T. Washington tried to stay out of the political light. He felt that political equality would come to America in time. He even gave speeches and said that African Americans weren't looking for equality. He said they just wanted to work hard with their hands to live a successful life. He hoped this would bring an end to the hate and violence. Many people, both black and white, supported him.

Team A: Supporters of Booker T. Washington

Member 3: Washington taught his principles to his students at Tuskegee Institute. He also helped other people in different states start other schools based on his beliefs. Many wealthy whites donated large amounts of money to Washington to run his now large and successful school.

Moderator 2: Team B, would you please comment about why people supported W.E.B. Du Bois, instead?

Team B: Supporters of W.E.B. Du Bois

Member 1: W.E.B. Du Bois wanted racism and segregation to stop immediately. He felt politics was a powerful tool to use to make these changes start to happen. As a writer, he shared his opinions with passion. Many blacks and whites supported his views.

Team B: Supporters of W.E.B. Du Bois

Member 2: He became the editor of *The Crisis*, the famous magazine of the NAACP. In the magazine, he wrote articles that spoke out strongly in support of integration. He used the power of the pen to tell everyone everywhere that all Americans, no matter what their race, should experience equal rights as citizens.

Team B: Supporters of W.E.B. Du Bois

Member 3: Du Bois was a champion for civil rights, long before Martin Luther King, Jr. and the Civil Rights Movement. Du Bois fought for civil rights in America. He also traveled through Europe and Africa in support of civil rights for people living in Africa. He was outspoken and passionate about bringing an end to racism.

Moderator 1: Now that we have heard both sides of the Great Debate, please comment on which side you think you would support if you lived during the years just after the Civil War. Team A, you may go first.

Team A: Supporters of Booker T. Washington

Member 1: I would support

_____

_____

_____

Team A: Supporters of Booker T. Washington

Member 2: In my opinion, I think

_____

_____

_____

Team A: Supporters of Booker T. Washington

Member 3: Since you're asking me, I'd say that

_____

_____

_____

Moderator 2: Team B, which side do you think you would support if you lived during that time?

Team B: Supporters of W.E.B. Du Bois

Member 1: I agree more with

_____

_____

_____

Team B: Supporters of W.E.B. Du Bois

Member 2: The thing I think is most important is

_____

_____

_____

Team B: Supporters of W.E.B. Du Bois

Member 3: I have to conclude that

_____

_____

_____

Moderator 1: As you can see, people still have opinions about the Great Debate.

Moderator 2: Think about the things you have learned today. Which side of the Great Debate would you support?

Possible Extensions

1. Before the play is performed, discuss the different points of view held between Booker T. Washington and W.E.B. Du Bois. Invite students to fill in the blanks on the script with their opinions. When they are prepared, assign roles and perform the play.

2. To learn more about Booker T. Washington's Tuskegee Institute and W.E.B. Du Bois and *The Crisis*, have students visit the following Web sites:

   • www.tuskegee.edu/

   • www.thecrisismagazine.com/

3. Discuss benefits and drawbacks of both sides of the Great Debate. Ask students to suggest other ways individuals as well as government leaders could have helped these years be a smoother transition for our country to progress from slavery to equal rights.

4. Have students write acrostics about Du Bois and Washington. Encourage them to choose words or phrases in their poems to represent what each man believed in and was known for. For the acrostic, students may use the last name of these leaders, or words such as NAACP, Tuskegee, or *Crisis*.

5. A glyph allows each student to express his or her opinion by creating a picture that conveys information based on items listed in a legend. Make a glyph together as a class to allow each of your students to share information about which side they support in the Great Debate. Make a bulletin board displaying a title about something both sides agreed on: Education = Success. Distribute construction paper and craft supplies for students to make their own schoolhouses by referring to the following legend. Mount the finished schoolhouses on the bulletin board and discuss the results. In the center of the board, hang a legend that explains the meaning of the glyph:

   • Red schoolhouse: supports Washington's view that it's best to learn industrial skills

   • Tan schoolhouse: supports Du Bois's view that it's important to pursue advanced academics

   • Yellow door: supports Washington's view of staying out of politics

   • Blue door: supports Du Bois's view of getting involved with politics

   • One window: supports Washington's view of hoping racism will stop over time

   • Two windows: supports Du Bois's view of demanding equal rights for all citizens now

   • One chimney: supports Washington's method of giving speeches mostly to white audiences

   • Two chimneys: supports Du Bois's view of writing news articles for most black audiences

6. Throughout the years, other important debates have taken place in America. Encourage students to research the following issues and learn more about these topics.

- In the late 1700s, Richard Allen and leaders at Mother Bethel A.M.E. in Philadelphia thought blacks should be ordained as church leaders.
- Leaders at St. George's United Methodist Church thought that only whites should be leaders and should oversee churches with predominantly black congregations.

- In the late 1700s, Prince Hall wanted to bring an end to the trans-Atlantic slave trade.
- Certain individuals, businesses, and politicians wanted the slave trade to continue.

- Benjamin Banneker stated that all people are equal, regardless of race.
- Thomas Jefferson voiced concerns that conveyed a hesitancy to admit equality among the races.

- James Forten, Robert Purvis, and other abolitionists wanted slavery to end in America.
- Politicians and individuals who supported slavery wanted to keep this institution intact.

- William Lloyd Garrison believed slavery should end by using powerful arguments to persuade Americans to take a stand against it.
- Frederick Douglass was eventually willing to take a militant stand to bring slavery to an end.

- Rosa Parks stood up for her civil rights by refusing to give up her seat to a white passenger on a bus.
- Local authorities in Montgomery, Alabama, and in many areas throughout the South supported Jim Crow, or segregation, laws.

- Martin Luther King, Jr. wanted full and equal rights for all citizens in America.
- Eugene "Bull" Conner wanted whites to maintain dominance over blacks.

Holidays

Juneteenth:
A Historic Day

Staging

Two narrators stand at a podium, desk, or music stand on the far left of the stage. A fictitious group of people (Prince, Bett, Cesar, Anna) stand in the center of the stage. Dinah (a fictitious woman) stands on the front right. Near her on the floor is her baby Liza. If you choose to use props, Liza can be represented by a life-sized doll on a blanket. Felix (a fictitious man) and Major-General Granger stand just behind the narrators and each move to center stage when it is their turn to speak. A crowd stands across the back of the stage. Place a stool in the center of the crowd for Cesar to sit on in Scene 3.

Characters

Narrators 1 and 2   Felix
Prince   Dinah
Bett   Crowd
Cesar   Major-General Granger
Anna

```
Crowd  X    X    X    X    X    X    X    X


                   Prince  Bett
                     X      X
            Cesar                Anna
              X                    X
General Granger
   X
Felix
   X



Narrators 1, 2                            Dinah
   X   X                                    X
```

Scene 1

Setting: Cotton field on plantation near Galveston, Texas

Narrator 1: President Abraham Lincoln issued the Emancipation Proclamation on January 1, 1863. This important document said that if any state did not come back into the Union by that date, every enslaved person living in that state would be forever free.

Narrator 2: During the Civil War, Union troops advanced throughout the southern states. Everywhere they went, they read the Emancipation Proclamation aloud to those who were enslaved. Entire plantations of slaves were set free, with great celebration and rejoicing.

Narrator 1: When Union troops tried to ride into Texas, however, Confederate soldiers forced them back. Therefore, the Emancipation Proclamation wasn't brought into Texas during the war. In fact, many plantation owners from other states sent slaves to live in Texas. They planned to never set them free. They tried not to let any slaves in Texas know that President Lincoln had written the Emancipation Proclamation.

Narrator 2: Finally, the Civil War was over. The North had won. On June 19, 1865, Union troops rode their horses into Texas. It was more than two years after the Emancipation Proclamation had been issued. Slavery was over in the United States of America. As we watch the Union troops ride into Galveston, Texas, we see a group of African Americans working on a nearby cotton plantation. This is a fictitious group of people. They are still enslaved. They don't know yet that on this day, their lives will change forever.

Prince: You better hoe those weeds faster, Bett. The overseer will take a whip to you if you don't.

Bett: I'm so tired today, though. I was up all night taking care of the master's new baby.

Cesar: Look over yonder! Who's running through the cotton fields? He's coming our way, but I can't make out who it is. These old eyes of mine are getting weaker every day.

Anna: Why, that's my Felix coming. Howdy! Felix! What news brings you here today? Why are your feet flying so fast?

Felix: The soldiers! They're coming!

Prince: What soldiers?

Felix: The Union soldiers of the United States of America. They're riding into Galveston.

Cesar: What difference does that make? Us folks don't have anything to do with soldiers.

Felix: These soldiers are different. Talk in Galveston says that these soldiers bring freedom.

Bett: You better not talk that way. The overseer will whip you till you can't stand.

Anna: Why are you speaking such foolishness?

Felix: There's talk in town. They say the Great War is over. They say the Union won. And we don't have to slave no more.

Anna: Is this true, Felix? Oh, could this be true?

Felix: I'm going to find out. If the soldiers say we're free, I want to be there to hear them. I don't want to miss my freedom.

Anna: I'll come with you.

Bett: Me, too!

Prince: Come on, Cesar. Put down that hoe. I'll help you walk to Galveston today.

Cesar: Someone best go tell my daughter Dinah. She's up at the house, cooking.

Bett: I'll go get her. Hurry! We don't want to miss our freedom!

Scene 2

Setting: Kitchen in master's house on cotton plantation near Galveston

Narrator 1: Bett dropped her hoe in the field where she was standing. She hurried as fast as she could up to the big house. There, in the kitchen, she found Dinah, cooking a pot of stew over the fire.

Bett: Dinah, put down that spoon. Freedom's coming.

Dinah: Bett, now I know you done gone pure crazy. What are you talking about?

Bett: Felix ran all the way out here to tell us. He said that soldiers are coming into Galveston. They're bringing freedom. Come on! We got to go, too. We can't miss our freedom.

Dinah: Sh-h-h. You know you'll get a whipping talking about freedom. Now be quiet. Sit and rest a spell. Get that crazy notion out of your head.

Bett: It's not crazy. Everyone from the fields is already gone into Galveston. Your pappy's gone. Anna's gone. Prince is gone. Now don't say another word. Put down that spoon.

Dinah: But you know I can't leave little Liza. She's sleeping there on the floor in the corner.

Bett: Bring your baby, too. If you get freedom, she'll get it, too. Come on! We don't want to miss our freedom!

Narrator 2: Afraid to go yet afraid to stay, Dinah finally dropped her spoon on the table. She picked up her baby in her arms and followed Bett out the door.

Scene 3

Setting: Street in Galveston, Texas

Narrator 1: A large crowd was gathering on the streets of the town. As Bett and Dinah hurried up, Dinah spotted Cesar sitting on a barrel.

Dinah: Pappy, is it true? Oh, could it be true? Is freedom really coming?

Cesar: That's what these old ears of mine are hearing.

Crowd: Here they come! Everyone, look! The Union soldiers are coming!

Narrator 2: A hush fell over the crowd as the soldiers rode their horses and marched into view. *Clip. Clop. Clip. Clop. Left. Right. Left. Right.* The soldiers marched down the street and stopped in the middle of town. The officer in front climbed down from his saddle. He disappeared inside a nearby house and reappeared standing on its balcony. He waved a paper high in the air.

Major-General Granger: I am here to issue General Order Number 3. Listen carefully to the words!

Narrator 1: General Granger read from the paper he held in his hand. The huge crowd of men, women, and children held their breaths and listened.

Major-General Granger: The people are informed that, in accordance with a proclamation from the Executive of the United States, all slaves are free. This involves an absolute equality of personal rights and rights of property between former masters and slaves; and the connection heretofore existing between them, becomes that between employer and hired labor. The Freedmen are advised to remain at their present homes, and work for wages. They are informed that they will not be allowed to collect at military posts; and that they will not be supported in idleness either there or elsewhere.

Narrator 2: For a moment, silence hung in the air. Then the crowd exploded with joy and cries of jubilee.

Crowd: Wahoo! We're free! We're forever free! Wahoo!

Narrator 1: Felix picked up Anna and swung her around in his arms.

Felix: Anna! We're free! That means we can get married proper now! We can stay in our own cabin, together, and not have to live on different plantations.

Anna: All our children will be free, too!

Narrator 2: Whoops and hollers of celebration filled the air. Dinah held baby Liza up high above her head.

Dinah: You're free, Liza! Hear that? You're forever free. No chains of slavery for you, sweet baby. No auction block's gonna tear you away from my arms. You're gonna grow up to be a fine lady. You're gonna go to school and learn to read and write. You're free!

Narrator 1: Church bells rang. Whistles blew. Hymns of praise were sung. Prince reached out and shook Cesar's hand. He kissed baby Liza on the cheek. Tears of joy streamed down Cesar's face.

Cesar: Our prayers have been answered. I never thought these old eyes would live to see this day. I'm free. My daughter's free. Even my grandbaby is free. Thank you, Lord Almighty! Freedom's come at last.

Prince: Freedom's here, and now I'm free to find my family. You might not see me in these parts any more. I'm heading over to Louisiana where they sold my wife and two sons. Freedom's here, and we're forever free!

Narrator 2: Someone hung the red, white, and blue American flag from the balcony of the house. The crowd of new American citizens gathered around the flag.

Crowd: *(singing)*

Oh, say, can you see, by the dawn's early light,
What so proudly we hailed at the twilight's last gleaming?
Whose broad stripes and bright stars, through the perilous fight,
O'er the ramparts we watched, were so gallantly streaming?
And the rockets' red glare, the bombs bursting in air,
Gave proof through the night that our flag was still there.
O say, does that star-spangled banner yet wave
O'er the land of the free and the home of the brave?

Narrator 1: Freedom came to Texas on June 19, 1865. This was the date that the last slaves in America were set free. Ever since that wonderful and glorious day, June 19, or Juneteenth as it came to be called, has been a time of jubilee and celebration.

Narrator 2: Every year, families came back to Texas to celebrate this important holiday. Barbecues filled the air with delicious aromas. Red foods such as watermelon and strawberry soda pop were served to remember the blood that was shed by those who were enslaved. Flags were flown.

Narrator 1: Prayer services were held. Parades marched joyfully through the streets. Sack races, baseball, and dancing were enjoyed by all. Finally, at the end of the day, fireworks exploded to bring the celebrations to an end.

Narrator 2: But Juneteenth will never end. In the late 1970s, Texas Representative Al Edwards worked to establish Juneteenth as an official holiday. It became a state holiday in Texas in 1980. People in towns and cities all across America celebrate Juneteenth today.

Possible Extensions

1. At many Juneteenth celebrations, the 13th Amendment is read aloud because it officially ended slavery in the United States of America. To view a copy of this 1865 amendment and print out the text for your students to read, visit the Web site: www.ourdocuments.gov/doc.php?flash=true&doc=40

2. Host a Juneteenth celebration at your school or in your community. Read a copy of General Order Number 3 or the 13th Amendment. Tell the story of how freedom reached Galveston Texas in 1865. Hold sack races, organize a baseball game, and have a parade. Fly the American flag and decorate floats or booths with paper flowers. Serve lots of delicious food including red strawberry soda pop and watermelon. Sing patriotic songs and conclude the day with fireworks.

3. Write a class letter with your students to send to city and state officials asking them to make Juneteenth an official holiday. Submit student letters to your local newspaper explaining the significance of this day in American history and what it means for all people to be free.

4. Slavery still exists in some countries today. With your students, research various organizations that try to stop modern-day slavery. Consider holding a fund drive to raise donations to help.

5. Students may enjoy learning more about Juneteenth by reading the following books:

   Juneteenth: A Celebration of Freedom by Charles A. Taylor (Greensboro, NC: Open Hand, 2002).

   Juneteenth: Freedom Day by Muriel Miller Branch (New York: Cobblehill, 1998).

   Juneteenth: Jubilee for Freedom by June Preszler (Mankato, MN: Capstone Press, 2007).

Science and Medicine

A Scientist Hall of Fame

Staging

Place a podium in the center front of the stage (a music stand or desk may be used instead). The emcee can stand at the podium during the entire play. Seat Louis T. Wright and Jane C. Wright in the front center of the stage, one on each side of the podium. Seat the remaining six scientists behind them in a slight semicircle across the stage so that they are facing the audience. When it is each character's turn, that person should walk up to the podium and speak. When finished, characters should return to their seats.

Characters

Emcee   Shirley Jackson
Benjamin Banneker   Katherine Johnson
George Washington Carver   Dr. Louis Wright
Charles Drew   Dr. Jane Wright
Jewel Plummer Cobb

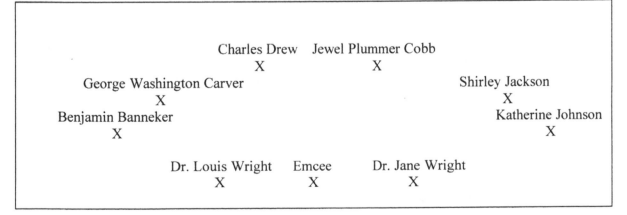

Note: Before performing this play, explain to students that these scientists are real people, but most did not all live at the same time or even know each other.

Emcee: Today we want to honor a father/daughter team of scientists in the field of medicine. We are hosting an imaginary Scientist Hall of Fame. We have invited other famous scientists from the past and present to speak at our imaginary ceremony in honor of our celebration as we add Dr. Louis Wright and his daughter Dr. Jane Wright to our special Hall of Fame. As our first guest today, please welcome Benjamin Banneker!

Benjamin Banneker: I am pleased to be here today to honor these two distinguished scientists. When Dr. Louis Wright founded the Harlem Hospital Cancer Research Foundation in 1948, it was a major step in offering hope to people everywhere who suffer from cancer. After her successful career in research at the foundation, his daughter Dr. Jane Wright eventually took over as director.

As a scientist myself, I understand the importance of research and how new findings can help people in everyday life. Along with my other scientific work, I spent many hours studying the stars, the planets, and the phases of the moon. Working out important mathematical equations, I was able to predict when the different phases of the moon would occur as well as the time the sun would rise and set each day in the year ahead. I knew this information would help farmers know when to plant which crops. I also knew this information would help sailors know when the tide was going out or coming in. I published this information in my almanacs over 200 years ago, during the 1790s.

Emcee: Thank you for being here at our Scientist Hall of Fame. Our next guest is George Washington Carver. Please welcome him today.

George Washington Carver: Thank you for inviting me to be here at this special event. I would like to point out that both Dr. Louis Wright and Dr. Jane Wright wrote important papers about their discoveries of how chemotherapy could help cancer patients. Other medical students and doctors used their research to help improve life for people diagnosed with cancer.

As a scientist, I also knew how important it was to write down my discoveries to share with other people. I was a chemist who did research with agricultural products such as the peanut and the sweet potato. I discovered over 300 useful products that could be made from peanuts as well as more than 100 products made from sweet potatoes. I wrote important papers about how to prepare the soil in a field to plant a crop such as peanuts. Then I explained in these papers how to grow the crop to produce a good yield. Finally, I described how to use the crop in many new and practical ways. My students read these papers in the science lab at Tuskegee Institute where I taught for many years. I also took these papers along with my portable school. I hitched a wagon to a mule and traveled from farm to farm, teaching poor farmers throughout the South better farming methods based on my research.

Emcee: Thank you for coming here to honor our two newest members of the Scientist Hall of Fame. Our next guest is Charles Drew. Please give him a warm welcome today.

Charles Drew: It's a pleasure to honor these two doctors and their contribution to the field of medicine. I would like to explain that around the time Dr. Louis Wright graduated from Harvard Medical School, World War I was being fought in Europe. As an officer in the Army Medical Corps, he used his medical skills to help wounded soldiers. After the war, he was hired to work at Harlem Hospital. During his medical career, he became an expert on head and skull injuries as well as fractures.

Years after Dr. Louis Wright was involved with World War I, my research got me involved with World War II. I wrote a paper called "Banked Blood" in which I explained how it could be possible to store large quantities of blood to be used when there was an emergency. There were so many wounded soldiers from Britain in World War II, that the British asked me to set up a blood bank to help. I organized a way for people to donate blood and developed better procedures for storing the blood. This blood was then sent to hospitals to help save the lives of wounded soldiers. Because of my success in Britain, America asked me to set up a similar program here in our country.

Emcee: Thank you for being a part of this special celebration. Also with us here is our next guest, Jewel Plummer Cobb. Please welcome her today.

Jewel Plummer Cobb: It's a joy to come here and honor this father-daughter team. As scientists, both understood the value of an education. In fact, Dr. Jane Wright became an instructor of research surgery at New York University Medical Center. She later was appointed dean of New York Medical College.

I was a cell biologist and spent many hours in research on cells. Along with my scientific career, I also held leadership positions at various universities. In 1981, I was appointed president of California State University at Fullerton.

Emcee: Thank you for being here at our Scientist Hall of Fame. Our next guest is Shirley Jackson. Please welcome her today.

Shirley Jackson: Thank you for inviting me to be here to celebrate! I would like to share how these two scientists have accomplished many firsts. Dr. Louis Wright was the first African American doctor to be hired at a New York City hospital, opening the doors for many others. Dr. Jane Wright was the first to make many important discoveries in her field of cancer research. I, too, accomplished many firsts in my career as a scientist. I was the first African American woman to get a Ph.D. from Massachusetts Institute of Technology. I worked in different research labs and became an expert in particle physics. In 1976, I was hired as a researcher for Bell Laboratories, where I spent many years of my career.

Emcee: Thank you for coming here to honor these two research scientists. Our next guest is Katherine Johnson. Please give her a warm welcome today.

Katherine Johnson: I appreciate being able to participate in this important day. I admire both doctors for their hard work to bring discrimination to an end in the scientific and medical community. Not only did Dr. Louis Wright overcome many obstacles from racism within the medical field where he worked, he was also active in the NAACP to help bring an end to racism within his community. As a woman in a career where mostly men worked, Dr. Jane Wright became an inspiration to women everywhere to work hard to achieve their dreams.

I, too, overcame segregation and discrimination to join the research division at NASA space center. I worked on important mathematical equations that helped get the *Apollo* spaceship ready for its successful flights to the moon. My career spanned thirty years in our nation's space program.

Emcee: Thank you for being here on this important day. I would now like to introduce to you our distinguished guests of honor. Please welcome Dr. Louis Wright and Dr. Jane Wright into our Scientist Hall of Fame!

Dr. Louis Wright and Dr. Jane Wright: Thank you! Thank you! Thank you very much!

Dr. Louis Wright: It is indeed a great honor to be here today. I worked hard to open doors to African Americans in the field of medicine. Also, my goal was to provide important answers through research to patients suffering from cancer or other conditions. The numerous awards and honors I have received show me how much people have valued my work.

Dr. Jane Wright: Thank you for having us here today. Along with the research I did in cancer, I knew how important it was to teach other doctors how to get involved in the research process. Together, through pursuing education and participating in research, we can help those who are in need. Together, we can inspire and encourage each other to do our best to change our world.

Possible Extensions

1. To learn more about the history of the colleges and universities these scientists were involved with, encourage students to look up the educational institutions on the Internet. Have students choose one college or university mentioned in the script and write a short report about its past, the courses it offers today, and why they might like to attend this college to earn a degree one day. Allow time for students to share their reports with the class. When finished, discuss the challenges and opportunities a college degree offers.

2. Take time to honor the people in the medical field in your own school or community. Have students write letters thanking them for their important contributions to the world.

3. To find ways your students can help with cancer research that Dr. Louis Wright and Dr. Jane Wright were instrumental in furthering, visit the American Cancer Society Web site at www.cancer.org/docroot/HOME/sup/sup_0.asp. Explore the options to donate, participate, and volunteer as a class.

4. For a variety of scientific experiments you can do in the classroom, visit the following Web sites for suggestions and lesson plans:
   - http://sciencespot.net/
   - www.accessexcellence.org/AE/AEC/AEF/1996/rogers_cell.html
   - www.pbs.org/wgbh/nova/teachers/activities/2809_genome.html

5. Divide students into small groups to play board games that encourage them to consider pursuing various careers or educational opportunities as they grow older. The board game Careers (by Parker Brothers) or The Game of Life (by Hasbro) are great games for this age.

Inventors

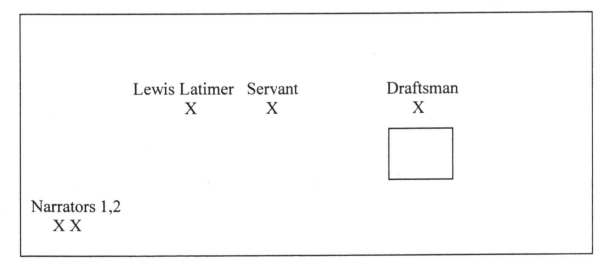

Lewis Latimer Helps Give Light to the World

Staging

Narrators may stand or sit on one side of the stage at the front. The draftsman can be sitting at a desk and can be drawing on a piece of paper. Lewis Latimer can enter the stage at the left and speak with the servant, who is already standing on stage at the beginning of the Scene 1. Characters not yet in a scene can wait offstage until it is their turn to enter and speak.

Characters

Narrators 1 and 2   Draftsman
Servant   Alexander Graham Bell
Lewis Latimer   Mary Latimer

```
Lewis Latimer    Servant              Draftsman
      X              X                     X
                                        ┌─────┐
                                        │     │
                                        └─────┘


Narrators 1,2
    X X
```

Note: Before performing this script, explain to the audience that Lewis Latimer, Mary Latimer, and Alexander Graham Bell were real people being portrayed in these fictitious scenes.

Scene 1

Setting: Street in Boston, just outside the office of patent lawyers Crosby and Gould

Narrator 1: Lewis Latimer was born in 1848, the son of George and Rebecca Latimer. His parents had run away from slavery in Virginia and escaped to Boston, Massachusetts. When his father was arrested with plans to return him to his master, abolitionists such as Frederick Douglass stepped forward in his defense. Funds were raised, George Latimer's freedom was purchased, and Lewis's father was set free.

Narrator 2: At the outbreak of the Civil War in 1861, young Lewis was eager to fight to help bring an end to slavery. At just fifteen years old, he signed up in the navy to serve as a cabin boy on the USS *Massasoit*.

Narrator 1: Finally, the Civil War brought slavery to an end. Lewis Latimer returned to Boston to look for a job.

Narrator 2: We find young Lewis walking the streets of Boston, searching for work. One morning, he knocked on the door of an office of patent lawyers Crosby and Gould.

Servant (opening the door): May I help you?

Lewis Latimer: I heard you were looking to hire an office boy.

Servant: That's right. We're looking for someone with good references, though.

Lewis Latimer: I've always been a hard worker for my employers. They'll be sure to give me a good recommendation.

Servant: Come on in, then. I'll show you around the office and introduce you to the owners.

Narrator 1: Lewis Latimer followed the servant inside the building. He was hired for general work and to run errands at the office. Every day, different inventors came to the office to discuss their inventions with the patent lawyers.

Narrator 2: Soon Lewis became interested in watching the draftsman make drawings of the inventor's ideas. He watched carefully to see how it was done. One day, he offered to make a drawing himself.

Lewis Latimer: Would you let me draw a picture of the new invention that someone brought in today?

Draftsman: Ha! You? You're just an office boy. I have a lot of work to do! You know I don't have time for such foolishness.

Lewis Latimer: I'd like to try. I've been watching how you do it. I bought myself my own set of drawing tools. Just like yours. I even bought a book and learned how it is done. I've practiced every night after I go home. Please—could I try drawing the invention myself?

Draftsman: It *would* be a big help to have you draw these inventions, too. Here's a piece of paper. Show me what you can do.

Narrator 1: Lewis sat down and picked up the drawing instruments. Very carefully, he began to draw details of the new invention.

Draftsman: I wouldn't have believed it if I didn't see you draw this with my very own eyes. You're good. You're very good!

Lewis Latimer: Thank you, sir.

Draftsman: I'll tell you what. Since I have such a big list of new inventions to draw today, you can help me.

Lewis Latimer: I brought my own tools to work today. I'll go get them and get started right away.

Narrator 2: From time to time, Lewis helped the draftsman draw pictures of the new inventions that came into the office. He soon became so good at drawing that he was hired as a draftsman, too. Eventually he became the chief draftsman at the office.

Scene 2

Setting: Late evening at the office of patent lawyers Crosby and Gould

Alexander Graham Bell: Are you available to help me tonight?

Lewis Latimer: Yes, I'm staying late at the office. I've been expecting you.

Alexander Graham Bell: Wonderful. I appreciate all the work you've already done to help me apply for a patent for my new invention. I think the telephone is going to be very popular. I think we could sell one to at least every train station in every city.

Lewis Latimer: Yes, I'm sure people will be eager to use it. Do you have the new part you want me to draw?

Alexander Graham Bell: Yes, here it is. I really appreciate you doing this. Your illustrations are always so clear, accurate, and precise in every detail. You're an outstanding draftsman!

Lewis Latimer: Thank you! I always try to do my best. I'll draw this tonight and have it ready for you right away. I know you want to apply for a patent for the telephone as soon as possible.

Narrator 1: Lewis Latimer illustrated the drawings for the various parts of Alexander Graham Bell's newest invention—the telephone. His detailed drafts helped Bell apply for the patent he eventually received.

Narrator 2: After a successful career working with the office of Crosby and Gould, Lewis Latimer left the company when there was a change in ownership. He moved to Bridgeport, Connecticut and got a job working for Hiram Maxim's company, the United States Electric Lighting Company. It was with Maxim's firm that Latimer did some of his most famous work as an inventor.

Scene 3

Setting: Home of Mary and Lewis Latimer

Lewis Latimer: Good evening, Mary!

Mary Latimer: Good evening, Lew. How was your day, today?

Lewis Latimer: Very, very productive. I've been hard at work experimenting on making a new filament for Edison's lightbulb.

Mary Latimer: I know you have to devote a lot of your time to that right now. Inventors all around the world are racing to be the first one to invent improvements to the lightbulb.

Lewis Latimer: Yes, the lightbulb that Thomas Edison designed is a marvelous invention. Unfortunately, it's expensive to make, and it burns out very quickly. But today I might have solved that problem!

Mary Latimer: What did you do?

Lewis Latimer: After hundreds of experiments, I finally designed a carbon filament that is inexpensive to produce. Also, it makes the lightbulb last much longer than Edison's original one.

Mary Latimer: This is wonderful news!

Lewis Latimer: Yes, I stayed late at the office so I could draw the design of it. I want to apply for the patent first thing in the morning.

Narrator 1: Lewis Latimer got the patent for his new invention. He is known today as the inventor of the first electric incandescent lamp that had a lightbulb with an improved carbon filament.

Narrator 2: Due to the great success with his lightbulb, he was hired to oversee installation of electric lights in various cities including New York, Philadelphia, Montreal, and London.

Narrator 1: Thomas Edison eventually offered Lewis Latimer a job. He worked as a chief draftsman. He also went to court frequently to defend Edison's patents. Lewis Latimer was one of the few members of the select group of engineers and inventors who became known as the famous Edison's Pioneers.

Narrator 2: By the end of his successful career as draftsman, engineer, and inventor, Lewis Latimer had also held positions as chief draftsman for both the General Electric and Westinghouse companies—also giants in the newly discovered industries of light and electricity. Lewis Latimer worked on the cutting edge of invention, industry, and new technology in America.

Possible Extensions

1. Invite students to learn more about Lewis Latimer by visiting the Web site http://edison.rutgers.edu/latimer/blueprnt.htm.

2. Divide students into small groups and assign each group a different African American inventor to research. Provide butcher paper for students to use to work together in their groups to draw a life-sized portrait of their inventor. Have them write a group report to share with the class and each make a model of their inventor's inventions to display.

3. Create a class book that is an encyclopedia of African American inventors from A to Z. Assign each student one or two inventors to research. On matching pieces of paper, instruct students to include the following: name of inventor, short biography, portrait if available, and illustration of invention. Bind pages together to form a book and display for students to read.

4. Host an Invention Day. Encourage students to create their own inventions and bring them in to share with the class. Let students vote on their favorites and give awards for such prizes as the most practical, the most creative, and the class favorite.

5. For more information about African American inventors, visit the following Web sites:

   • http://teacher.scholastic.com/activities/bhistory/inventors

   • http://inventors.about.com/library/blblackinventors.htm

   • www.swagga.com/inventors.htm

   • www.infoplease.com/spot/bhmscientists1.html

   • www.inventions.org/culture/african/index.html

6. To find biographies, activities, and science products for young inventors, visit the following Web sites:

   - www.invent.org

   - http://scientificsonline.com/

   - www.bkfk.com.

   - www.amazing-kids.org/kids3-00.htm

7. For competitions for kid inventors, check out the following Web sites:

   - www.nmoe.org/bubblewrap

   - www.futurecity.org/competition.shtm

   - www.usfirst.org/

   - http://school.discoveryeducation.com/sciencefaircentral/dysc/index.html

Sports

Jackie Robinson Integrates Baseball

Staging

Seat the sports announcer at a small table or desk at the front left of the stage. If you choose to add props, give the announcer a fake microphone painted black and made of a cardboard tube with a Styrofoam ball glued to the top. Seat the four baseball fans on stools across the center of the stage. Have them all face left, as if watching a game. The narrator may sit at the front right of the stage in this fictitious scene.

Characters

Sports Announcer   Baseball Fans 1, 2, 3, and 4
Narrator

```
                Baseball Fan 3        Baseball Fan 4
                      X                     X

                     Baseball Fan 1        Baseball Fan 2
                           X                     X




Sports Announcer                                          Narrator
      X                                                      X
```

Sports Announcer: Welcome to the 1955 World Series, baseball fans! The Brooklyn Dodgers have won the National League pennant before. They've played in the World Series before, but they've lost every time. They always say, "Wait till next year!" Well, this year, they're up against the New York Yankees. Will this year be another loss for the Dodgers? Or will they win the World Series for the very first time?

Baseball Fan 1: I've watched every single World Series game the Brooklyn Dodgers have played. I always keep my eye on Jackie Robinson. Number 42. He's the best! He's always been the best, even back in high school.

Baseball Fan 2: You knew Jackie Robinson in high school?

Baseball Fan 1: Sure! I'm from Pasadena, California. Just like Jackie. We both went to John Muir Technical High. Back then Jackie was already a star! He earned letters in football, basketball, baseball, and track.

Baseball Fan 3: I guess his family had a lot of money for him to be able to spend all his time in sports.

Baseball Fan 1: No, that's not how it was at all. Jackie was born on a small farm in Georgia. His parents were poor farmers—sharecroppers. His grandparents had been slaves. His family didn't have much money. Especially when his father deserted them soon after Jackie was born. His mother knew they wouldn't have a very successful life in Georgia. There was too much racism there. So she packed up her five children and moved the family out to Pasadena.

Baseball Fan 4: Was it better there?

Baseball Fan 1: Not much. Pasadena had Jim Crow laws, too. There was segregation. Jackie remembered going down to the community pool to go swimming on a hot summer day. But they wouldn't let him. Only whites were allowed to swim on most days. They told him to come back on a different day when they'd close the pool and let blacks in. Jackie knew those Jim Crow laws were no good.

Sports Announcer: It's a tie game now in the second inning with the score 2 to 2. It's going to be a close game today, folks. We're watching two great teams battle for the championship. Who will end up on top?

Baseball Fan 2: I'm cheering for the Dodgers to win. My favorite player has always been Number 42. I knew Jackie Robinson, too, before his days with the Brooklyn Dodgers. We were in college together. He told me lots of stories about his family. His mother had to do people's laundry and housecleaning to earn money. There were many days Jackie was hungry because they didn't have enough money for food. He told me about his brothers and sister, too. His big brother Mack was his hero.

Baseball Fan 1: What's so special about his brother Mack?

Baseball Fan 2: Mack was a track star! He came in second place behind Jesse Owens in the 1936 Olympics in Berlin. Mack won the silver medal for the 200-meter race. Jackie was in sports, too. In fact, there was one day Jackie said he'd never forget. He was in Pasadena Junior College. It was the spring of 1938 and both track season and baseball season were at the same time. Jackie's baseball team had their big game that day. If they won the game, they'd win the championship. But his track team had a meet that exact same day!

Baseball Fan 3: What did Jackie do?

Baseball Fan 2: He wanted to go to his track meet, too. So he drove all the way to the city where the track meet was held. Once there, he set a new record for the running broad jump! Then he drove all the way back to a different city for his baseball game. Once there, he led his team to win the championship!

Baseball Fan 4: Did Jackie just go to junior college?

Baseball Fan 2: No. After that, he went to UCLA. He lettered in four sports there, too. What an amazing athlete!

Sports Announcer: Jackie Robinson is on third base. Keep an eye on him, folks. Look! He's running toward home plate. Will he make it before Yogi Berra tags him out? He's there! Jackie Robinson just scored in the opening game of the World Series with his famous play—stealing home!

Baseball Fan 3: Way to go, 42! That's just like Jackie to steal home. I remember the very first time I ever saw him play. He stole home that day, too. It was in his first game playing for the Montreal Royals. That was the training team, or farm team, for the Brooklyn Dodgers.

Baseball Fan 1: It's quite a story how Jackie went from playing in the Negro Leagues to playing in the majors.

Baseball Fan 3: That's right! In the early 1940s, baseball was still segregated. Only white players played in the majors. Black players had to play in the Negro Leagues. After serving in the army, Jackie Robinson started playing baseball in the Negro Leagues. But Branch Rickey, President of the Brooklyn Dodgers, was determined to bring an end to racism in baseball. He came up with a plan to integrate baseball and that plan included Jackie Robinson.

Baseball Fan 2: Isn't it amazing how Branch Rickey picked Jackie Robinson?

Baseball Fan 3: It sure is. For about a year, Branch Rickey sent out baseball scouts to watch different players in the Negro Leagues. He knew that for his plan to integrate baseball to work, he needed a player who was great *on* the field and who was also great *off* the field. He needed a good baseball player and also a player with a good, strong character. This man had to be a role model so that doors would open for other African Americans to play baseball, too. Branch Rickey felt Jackie Robinson was the best man to integrate baseball.

Baseball Fan 4: Do you think it was hard for Jackie to join the majors?

Baseball Fan 3: It wasn't hard for him to play—he was one of the best. But it was hard to put up with all the racism. History was made on October 23, 1945, when Jackie Robinson signed the contract to play for the Montreal Royals, however. And from that moment on, it was very hard for Jackie. He got hate mail and death threats. Players on other teams hurt him by stepping on him with their baseball cleats. Pitchers tried to hit him when they pitched the ball. Many players and people in the crowds called him horrible racist names. Jackie stuck in there, though. He knew how important a role he had. By the time the first game of the Montreal Royals took place in Jersey City in 1946, Jackie was determined to play his best. It was an amazing game! Jackie Robinson hit a home run. He stole two bases. He batted in three runs. With Jackie Robinson on the field, the history of baseball would never be the same.

Sports Announcer: We're seeing some good baseball here today. Plenty of hits. Plenty of action. Plenty of excitement. Just listen to the crowds! We're getting close to the end of the opening game. New York Yankees are ahead. Brooklyn Dodgers are going to have to score to even up the game.

Baseball Fan 4: I remember the very first year Jackie played for the Royals. He led his team to the top! By the end of the season, they won the Little World Series. Fans poured out on the field to hug and congratulate Jackie. Baseball had a new star. America had a new hero. Branch Rickey knew he was ready for the Brooklyn Dodgers. Three new African American players joined the Montreal Royals: Catcher Roy Campanella and pitchers Don Newcombe and Roy Partlow. Jackie Robinson moved up and officially joined the Brooklyn Dodgers.

Baseball Fan 1: Things didn't get much easier for Jackie, did they?

Baseball Fan 4: Not at first. Some of the players for the Dodgers signed a petition saying they didn't want to play with an African American. Branch Rickey gave them a choice. He said they could either accept Jackie on their team or quit. Nobody quit. In fact, when his teammates started to hear all the racism against Jackie, they came to his defense. They knew Jackie had promised Branch Rickey he wouldn't get in a fight because it might ruin the chance for other black players to join the majors.

Baseball Fan 2: Wasn't Jackie's first year with the Dodgers amazing?

Baseball Fan 4: It sure was! Jackie led his team to victory after victory. By the end of the season, he won the Major League Rookie of the Year. He batted .297. He scored 125 runs. And he led the league in 29 stolen bases. An incredible record! Jackie became a symbol of inspiration, hope, and pride to everyone—both black and white.

Baseball Fan 3: Jackie's had quite a career, hasn't he?

Baseball Fan 4: He sure has! With Jackie Robinson on their team, the Brooklyn Dodgers have been one of the best in baseball. And now they're here today in the 1955 World Series. They lost in other World Series, but this time I know it will be different. This time I just know they'll win!

Sports Announcer: On no! The first game of the World Series is over. The Yankees beat the Dodgers 6 to 5. But the series isn't over yet. Be sure to come back for the next game. Will the Dodgers or the Yankees be baseball's new champions?

Narrator: That year, the Brooklyn Dodgers went on to win the 1955 World Series championship. The following year, Jackie Robinson was traded to the Giants, but announced that he would retire instead. He began a career as an executive of a large New York restaurant chain, Chock Full O'Nuts. Jackie Robinson was active in the Civil Rights Movement, worked for the National Association for the Advancement of Colored People, and became involved in politics. In 1962, this legendary baseball giant was elected into baseball's Hall of Fame.

Possible Extensions

1. Invite students to find out more about baseball greats by visiting the Negro Leagues Baseball Museum Web site at:www.nlbm.com. On the Web site they can read about the history of the leagues, keep up-to-date on current events concerning these giants in baseball, and learn more about each individual player. Students may also visit the National Baseball Hall of Fame & Museum Web site at: www.baseballhalloffame.org. By clicking on the link to Hall of Famers, they can explore short biographies and stats of players listed in the alphabetical roster. The link to the Negro Leaguers features biographies and stats of great ballplayers from teams existing in the Negro Leagues before Jackie Robinson integrated baseball. After searching through the Web site, invite students each to use a piece of construction paper to design a giant-sized baseball card honoring their favorite baseball player.

2. Hold a Four-Letter Sports Day for students to experience a little taste of what life was like for Jackie Robinson during high school and college days. Set up four stations with a modified game at each: tag football, basketball, baseball, and track and field. Rotate students from station to station until they take a turn at each sport. After the event, invite students to journal about their experience and write what they think it might have been like for Jackie Robinson to be a star in all four sports.

3. Discuss the strength and courage it took for Jackie Robinson to integrate baseball and stand up for what is right. Ask volunteers to describe tough situations in their own lives in which someone might be challenged to stand up for what is right. Talk about the different choices individuals have, and vote together on which action is best to take for each situation.

4. Distribute four-inch white construction paper circles to your students. Ask them to decorate it like a baseball and write on it one quality that they admire most about Jackie Robinson. Display the paper baseballs on a bulletin board titled "Jackie Robinson Scores!"

Literature

Phillis Wheatley and Famous Poets of Yesterday

Staging

Arrange the center of the stage to resemble a small classroom. In Scenes 1 and 3, have students sit on stools or on desks facing left to look at the teacher. On the right front of the stage, have Phillis Wheatley sitting in a chair holding a book, with the servant and Benjamin Franklin standing next to her. In Scene 2, the students and their teacher can move to stand near Phillis Wheatley. The narrator can stand at the left front of the stage.

Characters

Narrator	Servant
Teacher	Phillis Wheatley
Students 1, 2, 3, and 4	Benjamin Franklin

```
              Student      Student
                X            X

    Teacher
      X         Student    Student
                  X          X

                                              Benjamin
                                   Servant    Franklin
                                      X          X
    Narrator                            Phillis Wheatley
      X                                        X
```

Note: Explain to students that Phillis Wheatley was a real poet who became famous and traveled to London to oversee the publication of her book of poems. Many well-known dignitaries, including Benjamin Franklin, visited her to express their admiration.

Scene 1

Setting: Classroom

Narrator: Imagine being able to travel back in time! In these imaginary scenes, a group of students and their teacher travel back in time to visit a famous African American poet who actually lived in the past. This poet is real. But these scenes are just part of our imagination. Let's join the class now and travel … back in time!

Teacher: Good morning, class. For today's lesson, we will be studying about famous African American poets who actually lived in the past. I brought a special clock to help us.

Student 1: What's so special about that clock? It looks like a regular clock to me.

Teacher: If I move the hands of this clock backward, we will travel back in time.

Student 2: That sounds like fun! Let's try it!

Teacher: Okay. Which famous African American poet would you like to meet first?

Student 3: I'd like to meet the very first African American poet who ever published a book.

Teacher: That's Phillis Wheatley. She published her first book of poems when she was only nineteen years old! That was back in 1773.

Student 4: 1773! Will your clock take us that far back in time? That's more than 200 years ago.

Teacher: Let's try it and see. Get ready! Get set! Here we go-o-o-o!

Narrator: *(Flash lights on and off in the room. The students and their teacher should move to stand near Phillis Wheatley.)* What's happening? What's going on? They're traveling back in time!

Scene 2

Setting: Busy street in a well-to-do neighborhood

Student 1: This is so strange. We're not in our classroom anymore.

Student 2: We're in a big city! With people and horses and carriages riding past us on the street.

Student 3: Where are we? This doesn't look like America.

Teacher: It's not. We're in London, England in 1773.

Student 4: This is fun! That clock took us back in time.

Teacher: Come on! Let's go meet Phillis Wheatley.

Narrator: The group walked to a fancy apartment building and knocked on the door. A servant opened the door.

Servant: May I help you?

Teacher: Yes. We were hoping to meet Phillis Wheatley. Is she here?

Servant: Yes. Miss Wheatley is staying here during her visit to London. She's very busy, though. Many important people have to come to meet her. She's a very famous poet, you know.

Student 1: Do you think we could meet her, too? Today?

Servant: I don't know if you can meet her today or not. Someone very important has come to call on her already. Another American. Miss Wheatley is showing her new book to him right now.

Student 2: Do you think you could ask her if we could see her new book, too?

Servant: All right. Follow me. I'll take you in and ask.

Narrator: The group followed the servant inside. There, in an elegantly furnished room, sat a young woman holding a book on her lap. A man stood next to her.

Student 3: That man looks very familiar. I wonder who it is?

Student 4: Sh-h-h! You're talking too loudly. We don't want to interrupt them.

Servant: Please, Miss Wheatley. Another group of visitors has arrived. They are wondering if they can meet you and see your new book.

Phillis Wheatley: Of course! Mr. Franklin and I were just looking at it.

Benjamin Franklin: I'm a great admirer of Miss Wheatley, you know. I've read many of her poems already. They've been published in newspapers. She is an amazing writer for one so young and with such a difficult beginning.

Teacher: Thank you so much for allowing us a visit.

Narrator: Phillis Wheatley handed her book to the teacher, who showed it to the rest of the group.

Student 1: These poems are beautiful! How did you learn to write so well?

Student 2: Many of your poems seem to be about important events in American history, especially the American Revolution. Did you study history in school?

Phillis Wheatley: Actually, I am a slave. I was stolen from my parents when I was about seven years old. Torn away from my home in Africa, I was put upon a slave ship and brought to Boston. Once there, I was purchased and raised to be a domestic servant. But my owners allowed me to learn to read and write. I soon began to write poetry. I grew to love writing poetry more than anything else.

Student 3: But if you're a slave, how could you come here to London?

Student 4: How could you publish a book? And how could you get so famous?

Phillis Wheatley: When my poems started getting published in newspapers, they were very popular. I found people who supported my writing. A publisher in London agreed to publish my poems. My owners allowed me to travel here to promote my new book. In fact, after talking with abolitionists, my owners are planning to give me my freedom.

Benjamin Franklin: Phillis Wheatley's poems are extraordinary! Many of her poems are about important events going on in America and in the world. Other poems of hers are about famous people. She wrote such an amazing poem in honor of George Washington that he invited her to visit him. He wanted to meet this famous poet himself!

Teacher: What an honor it is to meet you ourselves. Thank you for allowing us to visit you today. We must go now, though.

Phillis Wheatley: Thank you for coming. It was a pleasure to meet you.

Narrator: The servant took the group to the door. Soon they were standing back on the busy street outside. The teacher held up the clock.

Teacher: It's time we head back to our classroom. I'm going to move the hands forward on this special clock. Get ready! Get set! Here we go-o-o-o!

Narrator: *(Flash lights on and off in the room. The students and their teacher should move back to their original positions in the classroom in Scene 1.)* They traveled forward in time. Soon they were back in their own classroom.

Scene 3

Setting: Classroom

Student 1: That was awesome! Can we do that again?

Teacher: Of course. Tomorrow we can travel back in time to visit another famous African American poet. Who would you like to see?

Student 2: Were there any other slaves who were famous poets?

Teacher: George Moses Horton was a slave, and he also became very famous as a poet. Even though he didn't know how to read or write, he composed many poems.

Student 3: How could he be a poet if he didn't know how to read or write?

Teacher: Horton wrote poems inside his head. He was known as the Southern Bard. A bard is a poet who recites poetry out loud to others. George Moses Horton dictated his poems to others, and they wrote them down. In fact, he even earned money writing poems. After he was done with his work for the week, he would walk to the nearby University of North Carolina. Students at the university paid him to write love poems for their sweethearts. He'd dictate the poems to them, and they wrote them down.

Student 4: Did he write all his poems like that?

Teacher: No. Eventually, someone noticed his extraordinary talent and taught him to read and write. He then published his poetry in antislavery newspapers and eventually into books. He hoped to earn enough money to purchase his freedom, but that never happened. He was a slave until the Civil War and the Emancipation Proclamation set him free.

Student 1: I'm glad he was finally set free.

Student 2: Me, too. Are there other famous African American poets we could travel back in time to visit, too?

Teacher: Of course! Tomorrow we can travel back to visit George Moses Horton. Who would you like to meet the next day?

Student 3: I'd like to meet someone from more modern times. Is there anyone who ever won the Pulitzer Prize?

Teacher: Yes. The first African American poet to win the Pulitzer Prize was Gwendolyn Brooks. Her book, *Annie Allen,* won the Pulitzer Prize in 1949.

Student 4: I'd like to learn more about her.

Teacher: Good! Her poems were a powerful voice during the Civil Rights Movement. She wrote many poems about important issues and famous African Americans during that time.

Narrator: Just then, the bell rang. It was time to go home. The students gathered up their books and backpacks. They got ready to leave.

Teacher: See you tomorrow. And remember—come prepared for our next adventure to travel back again in time!

Possible Extensions

1. Many of Phillis Wheatley's poems were about important current events of her day. Encourage students to choose a current event and write about it in a poem. Publish the poems together as a class book.

2. Phillis Wheatley also wrote poems to honor famous leaders in her day such as George Washington. Invite students to vote and choose one leader in your school, community, state, or nation to honor with a poem. Have students write original poems in honor of that leader. When finished, share the poems aloud with the class. To honor that leader, either send the individual a classroom set of poems, or choose one poem to represent the class and send.

3. Invite your students to write original Readers Theatre scripts to travel back in time and visit George Moses Horton, Gwendolyn Brooks, and other famous African American poets such as Lucy Terry (Prince), Jupiter Hammon, Armand Lanusse, Frances Ellen Watkins Harper, Langston Hughes, Rita Dove, and Maya Angelou. Provide resources for them to research these famous poets before they write their scripts.

4. Encourage students to choose favorite poems or portions of poems to memorize and recite before the class from books such as the following:

    The Black Bard of North Carolina: George Moses Horton and His Poetry, edited by Joan R. Sherman (Chapel Hill: The University of North Carolina Press, 1997).

    Bronzeville Boys and Girls by Gwendolyn Brooks (New York: Amistad, 2006).

    Complete Poems of Frances E.W. Harper, edited by Maryemma Graham (New York: Oxford University Press, 1988).

    Phillis Wheatley: Complete Writings, edited by Vincent Carretta (New York: Penguin Books, 2001).

    Selected Poems by Gwendolyn Brooks (New York: Harper Perennial Modern Classics, 2006).

5. Many cities and states have historical marker programs. To see the historical marker at the homesite of famous poet Frances E. W. Harper, visit Pennsylvania's Historical Marker Program at the Web site: www.phmc.state.pa.us/bah/DOH/categoryresults. asp?secid=31&category=Underground+Railroad&categorysubmit=Search+by+Categories. Read Frances E. W. Harper's marker's text with your students. Explain that historical markers give short but important details about a famous person or event associated with a historic place. Instruct students to write a historical marker that could be posted at the homesite of a famous African American poet they have researched. Provide paper and art supplies for students to make the historic markers. When finished, invite students to share their markers with the class and display them for others to see.

Visual Arts

Augusta Savage Shapes Her World

Staging

The narrator stands at a podium, desk, or music stand at the far left of the stage. Spread out and positioned across the stage are five stools or chairs. Have five students sit on the stools. Give them each a sign with the title of one of the sculptures listed in the play: Clay Duck, Marcus Garvey, W.E.B. Du Bois, *Gamin*, and *The Harp*. Three visitors walk from "sculpture" to "sculpture" as they look around in the imaginary art gallery.

Characters

Narrator   Bust of W.E.B. Du Bois
Visitors 1, 2, and 3   *Gamin*
Clay Duck   *The Harp*
Bust of Marcus Garvey

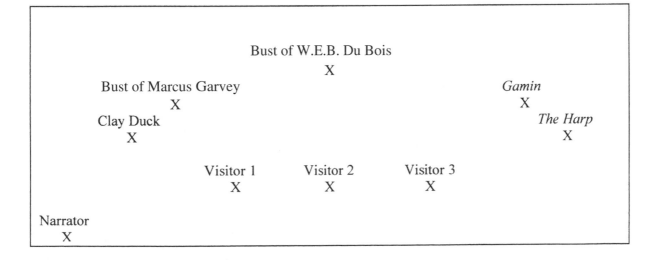

Narrator: Picture yourself visiting an imaginary art gallery. It's filled with sculptures created by the hands of a remarkable woman. As you walk around the gallery, you see amazing sculptures of people that almost look real. You see the looks on their faces, the pain and the hope. You see a giant harp made up of people, singing so proudly and so free. Why is this just an imaginary gallery, though? It's because most of these actual sculptures made by Augusta Savage have been destroyed or lost over time. Let's listen to these imaginary visitors to the gallery and find out more.

Visitor 1: There are so many interesting sculptures to look at. But isn't this strange! Over here is the figure of a small, clay duck. I wonder why this is here? Little duck, if you could talk, what would you tell us?

Clay Duck: I am made out of the rich, red clay of Florida. Small hands fashioned me out of the mud. While the rest of her fourteen brothers and sisters played in the mud and made simple mud pies, little Augusta started forming chickens and ducks. She saw things in the earth and formed me until I took shape. She gave me life, even though her parents did not approve.

Visitor 2: Why did her parents object to Augusta making things out of clay?

Clay Duck: Times were hard in the South during the 1890s when she was born. There were so many mouths to feed. Augusta's parents did not want her to grow up to be an artist. They wanted her to find work that would pay real money. Also, because of their religious beliefs, they did not think it was proper for people to make "graven images."

Visitor 3: What inspired Augusta to pursue her dreams? How did she grow up to become a famous sculptor?

Clay Duck: She got married when she was only fifteen and had a daughter a year later. Irene was her only child. Just a few years after that, her husband died. Augusta had to grow up early, but she still loved to make objects out of clay. A teacher noticed her talent and invited her to teach a high school clay modeling class. She entered some of her work in the Palm Beach County Fair and won a prize.

Visitor 1: Look at this piece over here. It's a sculpture of a famous leader named Marcus Garvey. I wonder why this is here? Marcus Garvey, if you could talk, what would you tell us?

Bust of Marcus Garvey: Augusta tried to make a living by creating busts of famous African Americans. They were so lifelike! They seemed so real! But it was hard to make a living as an artist in Florida. People encouraged Augusta to move to New York City and attend art school.

Visitor 2: Did she ever make it all the way north to New York City?

Bust of Marcus Garvey: It took a long time for Augusta to get enough courage and save enough money to travel North. Finally, in her late twenties, she got accepted at Cooper Union, an art school in New York City. She moved there to study sculpture. Soon she became well known in Harlem, a section of New York City where famous African American artists, writers, and leaders began to live. The Harlem Renaissance had begun. This era was a rebirth of African American culture that was influenced by the artistic efforts of amazing individuals, including Augusta Savage.

Visitor 3: What inspired Augusta to make a sculpture of Marcus Garvey?

Bust of Marcus Garvey: Garvey was the leader of an organization that wanted to create a free republic in Africa. Augusta created the sculpture of Garvey as one of many important leaders she portrayed in her work.

Visitor 1: Over here is another sculpture of an important leader. I recognize W.E.B. Du Bois, famous author, teacher, and scholar. W.E.B. Du Bois, if you could talk, what would you tell us?

Bust of W.E.B. Du Bois: I greatly admired Augusta's work. Once she became established in Harlem, she applied to study at an art program in France. But she was turned down—not because of her lack of talent. No, her talent as a sculptor was amazing! She was turned down because of her race.

Visitor 2: What happened then? Did she give up?

Bust of W.E.B. Du Bois: This terrible injustice brought Augusta great public support. I encouraged her to travel to Italy and study with great sculptors there. But even though she got a scholarship, she could not raise enough money to travel so far from home. Also, at this time, her parents became ill and other family tragedies occurred. Augusta moved her parents and most of her family to New York City so she could take care of them.

Visitor 3: Did Augusta ever make it to Paris to study?

Bust of W.E.B. Du Bois: Yes, her sculpture *Gamin* won the Julius Rosenwald Fellowship that let her study in France. Finally, she arrived in Paris in 1930. She studied sculpture and traveled throughout Europe. It was a wonderful time!

Visitor 1: Here is Augusta's famous sculpture named *Gamin.* Come look! It's of her nephew, a symbol of youth. *Gamin,* if you could talk, what would you tell us?

Gamin: As a sculptor, Augusta studied European art. Her fingers ached to create art that showed the world what life was like as an African American, however. When she created *Gamin,* in his face she captured a young, yet old-beyond-his-years expression. His face told of having to grow up too soon in a world that was full of hate and injustice and racism. Yet his face also portrayed a tender and expectant hope.

Visitor 2: Why were so many of her sculptures lost or destroyed?

Gamin: Augusta often made sculptures out of plaster and painted them. Plaster doesn't last very long. It crumbles and breaks easily. There wasn't enough money to cast most of her sculptures in bronze, which lasts a long time. But she was an artist during the Great Depression when most people did not have much money. Copies of some of her sculptures have been made. Also, there are photographs of some of her work.

Visitor 3: Did Augusta stay in Paris?

Gamin: No, she returned to New York City. She opened her own school in Harlem. It was called the Savage Studio of Arts and Crafts. One of her most famous students was Jacob Lawrence. She helped promote his career, and he became a great painter. Augusta once said about these years as an art teacher that if she could inspire young people to develop their talent, then her greatest work would live on through their art.

Visitor 1: Look over here! This sculpture is amazing! It's so huge! And it's in the shape of a harp. *Harp,* if you could talk, what would you tell us?

The Harp: In 1939, New York City hosted the World's Fair. Augusta Savage was one of four women, and the only black artist, who was paid to create an original work for the fair. She made a sixteen-foot-high sculpture of a harp. A choir represented the strings of the harp as they stood on the arm and hand of God. A man knelt in front and held a poem written by James Weldon Johnson called "Lift Every Voice and Sing." This sculpture symbolized the important contribution African Americans have made to the world of music.

Visitor 2: What happened to this sculpture?

The Harp: This sculpture became known as Augusta's most famous work. Sadly, it was destroyed after the fair was over. There are photographs, however, that show

Augusta working on its creation. Also, small copies of it can be found in collections or bought today.

Visitor 3: What were some of Augusta Savage's other great achievements?

The Harp: Augusta was an outstanding artist and accomplished many firsts. She was the first black member of the National Association of Women's Painters and Sculptors. During the Great Depression, she was the head of the Harlem Community Art Center, which was funded by the WPA Federal Art Project. At a time when many people were out of work, the Federal Art Project provided jobs for unemployed artists, educated children in the arts, and produced art for public buildings. Augusta Savage's life left an amazing legacy for others. Truly she is an inspiration for everyone to follow their dreams and "lift every voice and sing"!

Possible Extensions

1. Provide clay for your students to each make a bust of a famous African American. The individuals can be current or historic figures.

2. *The Harp* represented the significant contribution African Americans have made in the world of music. To research other important achievements in African American history, have students visit The African American Registry Web site at: http://www. aaregistry.com.

3. Augusta Savage dedicated many years of her life to help teach new artists. Organize a buddy system in which your students visit a kindergarten or first-grade classroom to help younger students create an art project. Use a project of your choice, or have them make simple puppets and perform Brer Rabbit stories based on Julius Lester's book *The Tales of Uncle Remus: The Adventures of Brer Rabbit.*

4. With her sculptures, Augusta Savage was known to create art representing her own cultural background. Encourage your students to choose an art medium such as sculpture, collage, painting, or drawing to create an art project reflecting their own cultural heritage.

Music

Marian Anderson's Voice Rings Out

Staging

The narrator may sit on a stool at the front right of the stage. The choir stands across the back of the stage. The other characters may all sit on stools or chairs along the left side of the stage. When it is their turn, they should walk to the center of the stage and talk with the other characters in that scene. Scene 1 begins with Marian Anderson and Aunt Mary talking together in the center of the stage.

Characters

Narrator
Aunt Mary
Marian
Choir Director
Choir

Church Members 1 and 2
Giuseppe Boghetti
Newsboy
Eleanor Roosevelt

```
        Choir  X    X    X    X    X    X    X    X


    Other              Marian Anderson  Aunt Mary
  performers                  X              X
    X
    X
    X
    X
    X
    X

                                               Narrator
                                                  X
```

Note: Be sure to explain that many characters in this fictitious performance represent real people such as Marian Anderson, Aunt Mary, Giuseppe Boghetti (Bo-GHETT-ee), and Eleanor Roosevelt.

Scene 1

Setting: Living room in the childhood home of Marian Anderson

Narrator: Ever since Marian was six years old, she loved to sing in the junior choir at her family's church, the Union Baptist Church in Philadelphia. Her aunt soon recognized how much people enjoyed listening to her rich, deep voice.

Aunt Mary: Come along, Marian! It's time for choir practice at the church.

Marian: I've been practicing all day.

Aunt Mary: My, you sing like a little bird! Every morning and all the day long.

Marian: At school yesterday, our class got to have singing lessons, too. That's my favorite day of the week at school.

Narrator: Aunt Mary took Marian to choir practice. As they walked along the street, Marian saw something on the ground. She bent down to pick it up.

Marian: Look at this, Aunt Mary! It's a paper with my picture on it.

Aunt Mary: Yes, I printed up a handbill for the church fundraiser. I'm planning on you singing for it. Folks love to hear you sing. Read what the paper says.

Marian: It says, "Come and hear our baby contralto sing."

Aunt Mary: Folks will pay good money to hear you sing with your beautiful voice. You can earn twenty-five or fifty cents.

Marian: So much money? Just for singing a song?

Aunt Mary: Yes, child. Other folks don't have a voice like yours. The good Lord gave you a gift. Use it well and you will go far.

Narrator: Marian and her aunt arrived at church. It was time for junior choir practice to start.

Choir director:	Good evening, Miss Mary and little Marian. Take your place with the other children in the choir, Marian. It's time to start singing.
Marian and Choir:	*(singing or reading slowly)* Deep river, My home is over Jordan. Deep river, Lord, I want to cross over into campground. Deep river, My home is over Jordan. Deep river, Lord, I want to cross over into campground.

Scene 2

Setting: Union Baptist Church in Philadelphia

Narrator:	Marian's church always supported her singing career. As she grew older, she sang at many church events. In 1919, she traveled to Atlantic City, where she sang at the National Baptist Convention.
Church Member 1:	It's too bad that Marian's father died when she was so young.
Church Member 2:	Yes, her family is so poor. Her mother works hard to support the family now. And Marian hardly has enough money even to buy a dress for her concerts.
Church Member 1:	She gives most of the money she earns to her mother and sisters to help out, doesn't she?
Church Member 2:	Yes. Oh look! Here she comes now.
Marian:	Good morning!
Church Members 1 and 2:	Good morning, Marian.
Church Member 1:	I heard you applied to music school here in Philadelphia.
Marian:	Yes, but they told me they don't allow black people in their school.

Church Member 2: That's terrible! You should take private lessons, then. Your voice is so beautiful you could take lessons from the famous teacher, Giuseppe Boghetti.

Marian: Oh, no! I'll never have enough money to take lessons from him. His lessons cost hundreds of dollars. He's one of the best teachers there is.

Church Member 1: If he's the best, then we'll see to it that you get the money to take lessons from him.

Church Member 2: We'll hold a church fundraiser! Everyone will give money to help you get the training your voice deserves.

Narrator: A church fundraiser was held. Everyone came to the concert. The church raised hundreds of dollars, enough for her to take private lessons. That night, Marian sang with all her heart.

Marian and Choir: *(singing or reading slowly)*
He's got the whole world in His hands,
He's got the big round world in His hands,
He's got the wide world in His hands,
He's got the whole world in His hands.
He's got the little bitsy baby in His hands,
He's got the little bitsy baby in His hands,
He's got the little bitsy baby in His hands,
He's got the whole world in His hands.
He's got everybody in His hands,
He's got everybody in His hands,
He's got everybody here right in His hands,
He's got the whole world in His hands.

Scene 3

Setting: Home of famous singing instructor, Giuseppe Boghetti

Narrator: Marian took lessons from Giuseppe Boghetti. He taught her how a singer was supposed to breathe to make the songs more powerful and rich. He taught her songs in German, Italian, and French, just like famous singers learned to sing.

Giuseppe Boghetti: Marian, your concert went well last night.

Marian: Yes, the university hall was filled. So many people came! I'm making enough money from my concerts now that my mother can stop working.

Giuseppe Boghetti: This is wonderful news! Your singing has been getting better and better every day. I think you should consider studying with teachers in Europe now.

Marian: Do you think I'm ready to travel to Europe?

Giuseppe Boghetti: Yes. I think you have the most beautiful voice in the world.

Narrator: Soon Marian traveled to Europe. She studied different languages and learned entire new sets of songs to sing. She sang in London, Berlin, Paris, and Moscow. She sang to sold-out crowds in Sweden, Finland, and Denmark. She sang before kings and queens. She sang back home in the United States and in South America. She became one of the most famous singers in the world. And then one day, a concert was planned for her to sing at Constitution Hall in Washington, D.C.

Newsboy: Get your news! Read all about it! The Daughters of the American Revolution refuse to let Marian Anderson sing at Constitution Hall. They say only whites are allowed to perform there. Read all about it!

Eleanor Roosevelt: This is terrible news. Miss Anderson has sung in royal palaces in countries all around the world. Yet her own country refuses to allow her to sing in its capital. I must do something about this.

Newsboy: Get your news! Read all about it! Eleanor Roosevelt resigns her membership from the Daughters of the American Revolution. Marian Anderson invited to sing at the Lincoln Memorial instead.

Narrator: That is how, on Easter Sunday in 1939, 75,000 people gathered to hear Marian Anderson sing in front of the Lincoln Memorial. It was a turning point in American history for racial equality and equal rights.

Marian and Choir: *(singing or reading slowly)*
My country, 'tis of thee,
Sweet land of liberty,
Of thee I sing.
Land where my fathers died,
Land of the pilgrims' pride,
From every mountainside let freedom ring!

Possible Extensions

1. If students are unfamiliar with the melody of the spirituals in this play, search the Web site www.amazon.com to locate the CD *Spirituals* by Marian Anderson. Before the play is performed, invite students to listen to Amazon's online clips of "Deep River" and "He's Got the Whole World in His Hands." There are also a wide range of Internet video clips, DVDs, and CDs available of Marian Anderson such as *Marian Anderson: A Portrait in Music* and *Jan Peerce, Marian Anderson & Andres Segovia*. Also check at your local library. Together with your students, watch or listen to her sing.

2. Divide students into small groups. Assign each group one spiritual to research and learn to sing. When finished, have each group share about the spiritual they studied and sing it in front of the class. To listen to the tunes of various spirituals and discover the history behind them, have students visit the Web site: www.negrospirituals.com.

3. Marian Anderson participated in various school performances that helped her gain confidence in her natural singing abilities. Host a talent show to showcase your students' gifts and abilities. Take sign-ups for participants. Over a period of several weeks, allow time for students to practice on a stage at school. Schedule a day for other classes to watch the dress rehearsal, then invite family and friends to enjoy the show.

The Civil Rights Movement

The March on Washington

Staging

The marchers should be standing all across the back of the stage. If you choose to add props, they can each carry a placard of the various statements they will proclaim. The rest of the characters should be mixed in among the marchers. When it is each character's turn to speak, that person should walk forward and stand next to the reporter, who is at the front and center of the stage, and then return to stand with the marchers when finished. The reporter can be holding a microphone (made of a cardboard tube with a Styrofoam ball glued on the top) in this fictitious scene.

Characters

Reporter	Celebrity
Marchers	Grandparent
Student	Teacher
Lawyer	Minister
Truck Driver	

Marchers	X	X	X	X	X	X	X	X	X	X	X	X
Student	Lawyer		Truck Driver		Celebrity		Grandparent		Teacher		Minister	
X	X		X		X		X		X		X	

Reporter
X

Reporter: Today is August 28, 1963. We are gathered here in the capital of our nation, Washington, D.C. What an amazing sight this is! A quarter of a million people have assembled peacefully today—blacks and whites, young and old, rich and poor. Together they are telling the world that it's time for America to be a land of freedom and equal rights for everyone.

Marchers: If you're not against discrimination, you're not for freedom.

Reporter: Standing here with me today is a student. Why did you come to join the March on Washington and how did you get here?

Student: I'm from North Carolina. I came by bus with a group of friends from my school. All the way here, we sang freedom songs. When our bus pulled into the station, they told us that hundreds of buses had been arriving all morning. Some folks came by trains from as far away as Georgia. An airplane of celebrities flew in from Hollywood. One guy even skated all the way here from Chicago on roller skates. The reason I came is the same reason everyone else came. It's time to take a stand against discrimination. Everyone is equal and everyone should have equal rights. This is the land of the free, but not everyone has had the freedom to do as they choose.

Marchers: We march for effective civil rights laws now!

Reporter: Standing here with me now is a lawyer. Can you tell us what makes this demonstration different from any other demonstration that's ever been held at the capital?

Lawyer: Right now there is a civil rights bill in Congress. President John F. Kennedy supports it. And if it gets voted in, racial discrimination will be against the law. All these people have come here today to let our political leaders know that this bill is important. We need effective civil rights laws to make sure everyone's rights are protected in America no matter what color their skin is.

Marchers: We march for jobs for all now!

Reporter: Standing here with me is a truck driver. What has this day been like for you and why are you here with the marchers?

Truck Driver: This morning, we listened to famous singers sing freedom songs on the stage near the Washington Monument. This monument is a symbol of our Constitution that says all men and women are created equal. Yet so many people in our country can't get equal jobs, equal pay, or equal housing because of the color of their skin. One hundred years ago, President Lincoln signed the Emancipation Proclamation. This important document said that slaves were forever free. But even after one hundred years, many people still don't experience equality and freedom. I came here today to tell the world that it's time for this to change.

Marchers: We march for first-class citizenship now!

Reporter: Standing here with me now is a celebrity. Why did someone as rich and famous as you come to the March on Washington today?

Celebrity: I live in California, but as a singer, I travel through every state. When I visit some states, I can't stay in certain hotels. I can't eat in certain restaurants. I can't even use certain bathrooms. People living in other parts of the country don't realize that many states still treat African Americans as if they were slaves. I should be able to choose the hotel I want to stay at and go to the store where I want to shop, but not just because I'm rich and famous. Everyone should be able to live freely and be treated as a first-class citizen in America.

Marchers: We demand voting rights now!

Reporter: Standing here with me now is a grandparent. Can you tell us what the most important thing is for you here today?

Grandparent: I've lived a long time. My parents were slaves. After the Civil War ended, they got their freedom. For the first time in their lives, they were able to vote. But not for long. Soon those voting rights were taken away from black citizens either through threats or with new laws that made it impossible for African Americans to vote. The power of the vote gives each person a voice to make a difference in our world. Today, each person here is a silent, but powerful voice. Together we are telling the nation that it's time to give us our voting rights, our equal rights, and our full rights as Americans.

Marchers: We march for integrated schools now!

Reporter: Standing here with me now is a teacher. How do you think the events of this day will affect our nation?

Teacher: Today is a turning point in history. This is the biggest demonstration of this kind that our nation has ever seen. Blacks and whites have joined together to show the world we can overcome any prejudice and racism that exists in our country today. We won't stop until children of all races are free to play in the park together. We won't keep silent until children of all races are free to go to school together. We won't quit until children are free to be friends with each other no matter what color their skin is.

Marchers: We demand an end to bias now!

Reporter: Standing here with me now is a minister. Can you tell me what today means to everyone all across the nation watching this event on their TV in their own living rooms?

Minister: The prayers and speeches given today at the Lincoln Memorial are being heard by people watching the news all across the nation. Dr. Martin Luther King's powerful speech, "I Have A Dream," will inspire everyone to look forward to the future—a future where all his dreams will come true and bias against race will end. Truly this day will be remembered for the speech Dr. King gave and for the people who came to show their support for equal rights. My hope is that one day every American will echo Dr. King's words, "Free at last! Free at last! Thank God Almighty, we are free at last!"

Possible Extensions

1. Write a list of vocabulary words on the board such as *discrimination, demonstration, rights, racism, citizenship, integration, segregation, prejudice,* and *bias.* Have students look up the meaning of each word. Provide graph or plain paper for students to use to make a crossword puzzle from the vocabulary words, and list the definitions as the clues. Invite them to trade with a partner to complete the puzzles.

2. Discuss conditions existing in the nation during the 1950s and 1960s that caused discrimination, segregation, and racism. Then discuss how these conditions led to the Civil Rights Movment. Show pictures of marchers carrying placards on the March on Washington. Invite students to state which placard they would have chosen to carry during the march and explain why. Visit the following Web sites to see photographs of the Marchers:

   • www.pbs.org/wgbh/amex/eyesontheprize/story/img_08_washington_03.html

   • www.pbs.org/wgbh/amex/eyesontheprize/story/img_08_washington_07.html

   • www.africanafrican.com/negroartist/CIVIL%20RIGHTS%20IMAGERY/index.html

3. Look at a map of the United States with your students. Point out various routes and talk about different forms of transportation students from your school could take to go to the capital if the March on Washington were held today.

4. Divide students into five groups. Instruct each group to be a "mock" planning committee with the responsibility of organizing and planning the March on Washington.

   • Group 1: Schedule trains, airplanes, buses, and carpools from all across the nation to arrive early in the morning and leave before dusk the same day. Determine the numbers they would need, from which cities they would depart, and at which stations they would arrive near Washington, D.C.

   • Group 2: Organize police, first aid, food, drinking fountains, and portable toilets for 250,000 people to assemble in front of the Lincoln Memorial. Draw a map of the area to show where to position each one.

   • Group 3: Invite television and newspaper reporters from across the nation to cover the event. Make a list of the major networks they would contact.

   • Group 4: Plan the morning schedule of entertainment and singers at the Washington Monument. Design a program for the event.

   • Group 5: Plan the afternoon schedule of speakers and singers at the Lincoln Memorial. Design a program for the event.

Teacher Resources

Books about African American History

Appiah, Kwame Anthony, and Henry Louis Gates, Jr. *Africana.* New York: Basic Civitas Books, 1999.

Cantor, George. *Historic Landmarks of Black America.* Detroit: Gale Research, 1991.

Ciment, James. *Atlas of African-American History.* New York: Checkmark Books, 2001.

Dodson, Howard, et al. *Jubilee.* Washington, DC: National Geographic, 2002.

Editors of Time-Life Books. *African Americans Voices of Triumph: Perseverance, Leadership, and Creative Fire.* Alexandria, VA: Time-Life Books, 1994.

Gates, Henry Louis, Jr., and Evelyn Brooks Higginbotham, Editors. *The African American National Biography.* Oxford University Press, 2008.

Gates, Henry Louis, Jr., and Cornel West. *The African American Century.* New York: The Free Press, 2000.

Harley, Sharon. *The Timetables of African-American History.* New York: Simon & Schuster, 1995.

Hine, Darlene Clark. *Black Women in America: An Historical Encyclopedia.* Brooklyn, NY: Carlson, 1993.

Hopkins, Lee Bennett. *Important Dates in Afro-American History.* New York: Franklin Watts, 1969.

Hornsby, Alton, Jr. *Chronology of African-American History.* Detroit: Gale Research, 1991.

Newman, Richard. *African American Quotations.* New York: Checkmark Books, 2000.

Salzman, Jack. *The African-American Experience.* New York: Macmillan Library Reference USA, 1993.

Smith, Jessie Carney. *Black Firsts.* Detroit: Visible Ink Press, 1994.

Smith, Jessie Carney. *Notable Black American Men.* Detroit: Gale Group, 1999.

Williams, Michael W., Ed. *The African American Encyclopedia.* Volumes 1–8. New York: Marshall Cavendish, 1993.

Student Resources

Altman, Susan. *The Encyclopedia of African-American Heritage.* New York: Facts on File, 1997.

Green, Richard L., et al. *A Salute to Black History Series.* Chicago: Empak, 1996.

Hughes, Langston, et al. *A Pictorial History of African Americans.* New York: Crown, 1995.

Patrick, Diane. *The New York Public Library Amazing African American History.* New York: John Wiley & Sons, 1998.

Rennett, Richard, Ed. *Black Americans of Achievement Series*. Philadelphia: Chelsea House, 1992.

Sanders, Nancy I. *A Kid's Guide to African American History*. Chicago: Chicago Review Press, 2007.

Sanders, Nancy I. *D is for Drinking Gourd: An African American Alphabet*. Chelsea, MI: Sleeping Bear Press, 2007.

Smith, Sande, Ed. *Who's Who in African-American History*. New York: Smithmark, 1994.

Stewart, Jeffrey C. *1001 Things Everyone Should Know about African American History*. New York: Main Street Books, 1996.

Web Sites

www.aakulturezone.com/kidz/index.html

> An interactive Web site for students to learn more about African American culture including biographies from A to Z, online cards to send, photographs to view, timelines, and suggested books.

www.headbone.com/derby/escape/

> An online interactive investigation into the underground railroad complete with teacher guides for Grades 4–8.

www.kn.pacbell.com/wired/BHM/index.html

> A host of in-depth studies for older students to explore on a variety of topics regarding the history of African Americans.

www.loc.gov/exhibits/african/intro.html

> An online exhibit of the Library of Congress' large collection of African American history covering Colonization, Abolition, Migration, and the WPA.

www.teachervision.fen.com/african-americans/resource/4429.html

> An encyclopedia listing prominent African Americans from A to Z, with downloadable coloring pages, teachers' guides, and links to resources on African American history covering a comprehensive range of grade levels.

Selected Bibliography

Books

Abdul-Jabbar, Kareem, and Alan Steinberg. *Black Profiles in Courage*. New York: William Morrow, 1996.

Adams, James Truslow, Ed. *Album of American History*. Volumes 1–5. New York: Charles Scribner's Sons, 1946.

Alexander, E. Curtis. *Richard Allen*. New York: ECA Associates, 1985.

Altman, Susan. *The Encyclopedia of African-American Heritage*. New York: Facts on File, 1997.

Andrews, William L., and William S. McFeely, Eds. *Narrative of the Life of Frederick Douglass, an American Slave, Written by Himself*. New York: W. W. Norton, 1997.

Appiah, Kwame Anthony, and Henry Louis Gates, Jr. *Africana*. New York: Basic Civitas Books, 1999.

Bennett, Lerone, Jr. *Before the Mayflower*. New York: Penguin Books, 1988.

Billington, Ray Allen, Ed. *The Journal of Charlotte L. Forten*. New York: W. W. Norton, 1953.

Blanco, Richard L., Ed. *The American Revolution*. New York: Garland, 1993.

Brady, Paul L. *The Black Badge*. Los Angeles, CA: Milligan Books, 2005.

Branch, Muriel Miller. *Juneteenth: Freedom Day*. New York: Cobblehill, 1998.

Branch, Taylor. *Parting the Waters*. New York: Simon & Schuster, 1988.

Brill, Marlene Targ. *Barack Obama*. Minneapolis, MN: Millbrook Press, 2006.

Brown, Hallie Q. *Homespun Heroines*. Xenia, Ohio: Aldene, 1926. Accessed on http://docsouth. unc.edu/.

Buckley, Gail. *American Patriots*. New York: Random House, 2001.

Burton, Art T. *Black Gun, Silver Star*. Lincoln: University of Nebraska Press, 2006.

Chidsey, Donald Barr. *The Siege of Boston*. New York: Crown, 1966.

Child, L. Maria. *The Freedmen's Book*. Boston: Ticknor and Fields, 1865.

Christian, Charles M. *Black Saga*. Washington, DC: Counterpoint, 1999.

Ciment, James. *Atlas of African-American History*. New York: Checkmark Books, 2001.

Collins, Charles M., and David Cohen. 1993. *The African Americans: A Celebration of Achievement*. New York: Viking Studio Books.

Compton's Encyclopedia. Volumes 1–26. Chicago: Compton's Learning Company, 1992.

Cox, Clinton. *Come All You Brave Soldiers: Blacks in the Revolutionary War*. New York: Scholastic, 2002.

Crawford, Richard, Ed. *The Civil War Songbook*. New York: Dover, 1977.

Crew, Spencer R. *Field to Factory: Afro-American Migration 1915–1940*. Washington, DC: Smithsonian Institution, 1987.

Curtis, Nancy C. *Black Heritage Sites: The North, The South*. New York: The New Press, 1996.

Davis, William C. *Rebels & Yankees: The Fighting Men of the Civil War, The Battlefields of the Civil War, The Commanders of the Civil War*. London: Salamander Books, 1999.

Davis, William C., and Bell L. Wiley, Eds. *Civil War Album: Complete Photographic History of the Civil War*. New York: Tess Press, 2000.

Dougherty, Steve. *Hopes and Dreams: The Story of Barack Obama*. New York: Black Dog & Leventhal, 2007.

Douglass, William. *Annals of the First African Church*. Philadelphia: King and Baird, 1862. Accessed on http://quod.lib.umich.edu.

Editors of Time-Life Books. *African Americans: Voices of Triumph: Perseverance, Leadership*, and *Creative Fire*. Alexandria, VA: Time-Life Books, 1994.

Edwards, Roberta. *Barack Obama*. New York: Grosset & Dunlap, 2008.

Fishel, Leslie H., Jr., and Benjamin Quarles. *The Negro American: A Documentary History*. Glenview, IL: Scott Foresman, 1967.

Freedman, Russell. *The Voice That Challenged a Nation*. New York: Clarion Books, 2004.

Gates, Henry Louis, Jr., and Cornel West. *The African American Century*. New York: The Free Press, 2000.

George, Carol V. R. *Segregated Sabbaths*. New York: Oxford University Press, 1973.

George, Linda, and Charles George. *The Tuskegee Airmen*. New York: Children's Press, 2001.

Grabowski, John. *Jackie Robinson*. New York: Chelsea House, 1991.

Graham, Maryemma, Ed. *Complete Poems of Frances E. W. Harper*. New York: Oxford University Press, 1988.

Green, Richard L., et al. *A Salute to Historic Black Women*. Chicago: Empak, 1996.

Harley, Sharon. *The Timetables of African-American History*. New York: Simon & Schuster, 1995.

Haskins, Jim. *Black Eagles*. New York: Scholastic, 1995.

Haskins, Jim. *The Day Martin Luther King, Jr., was Shot*. New York: Scholastic, 1992.

Hedgepeth, Chester M., Jr. *Twentieth-Century African-American Writers and Artists*. Chicago: American Library Association, 1991.

Hine, Darlene Clark. *Black Women in America: An Historical Encyclopedia*. Brooklyn, NY: Carlson, 1993.

Hine, Darlene Clark. *Facts on File Encyclopedia of Black Women in America: Dance, Sports, and Visual Arts*. New York: Facts on File, 1997.

Hine, Darlene Clark. *Facts on File Encyclopedia of Black Women in America: The Early Years, 1619–1899*. New York: Facts on File, 1997.

Hine, Darlene Clark. *Facts on File Encyclopedia of Black Women in America: Literature*. New York: Facts on File, 1997.

Hine, Darlene Clark. *Facts on File Encyclopedia of Black Women in America: Music*. New York: Facts on File, 1997.

Igus, Toyomi, Ed. *Great Women in the Struggle*. Orange, NJ: Just Us Books, 1991.

Jackson, Blyden. *A History of Afro-American Literature, Volume 1*. Baton Rouge: Louisiana State University Press, 1989.

Jordan, Robert. *The Civil War*. Washington, DC: National Geographic Society, 1975.

Kaplan, Sidney, and Emma Nogrady Kaplan. *The Black Presence in the Era of the American Revolution*. Amherst: University of Massachusetts Press, 1989.

Klots, Steve. *Richard Allen*. New York: Chelsea House, 1991.

Lanker, Brian. *I Dream a World*. New York: Stewart, Tabori & Chang, 1989.

Leckie, Robert. *The Wars of America*. New York: Harper & Row, 1968.

Levenson, Dorothy. *The First Book of the Civil War*. New York: Franklin Watts, 1968.

Levine, Ellen. *... If You Lived at the Time of Martin Luther King*. New York: Scholastic, 1990.

Levy, Peter B. *The Civil Rights Movement*. Westport, CT: Greenwood Press, 1998.

Levy, Peter B., Ed. *Documentary History of the Modern Civil Rights Movement*. Westport, CT: Greenwood Press, 1992.

Loewenbert, Bert James, and Ruth Bogin. *Black Women in Nineteenth-Century American Life*. University Park: Pennsylvania State University Press, 1976.

Lowery, Charles D., and John F. Marszalek. *Encyclopedia of African-American Civil Rights*. Westport, CT: Greenwood Press, 1992.

Mathews, Marcia M. *Richard Allen*. Baltimore: Helicon, 1963.

McDowell, Bart. *The Revolutionary War*. Washington, DC: National Geographic Society, 1972.

McGovern, James R. *Black Eagle*. Tuscaloosa: University of Alabama Press, 1985.

McKissack, Patricia, and McKissack, Fredrick. *The Royal Kingdoms of Ghana, Mali, and Songhay*. New York: Henry Holt, 1994.

McMickle, Marvin A. *An Encyclopedia of African American Christian Heritage*. Valley Forge, PA: Judson Press, 2002.

Meltzer, Milton, Ed. *The Black Americans: A History in Their Own Words*. New York: HarperCollins, 1984.

Miles, Johnnie H., Juanita J. Davis, Sharon E. Ferguson-Roberts, and Rita G. Giles. *Almanac of African American Heritage*. Paramus, NJ: Prentice Hall Press, 2001.

Morris, Richard B., Ed. *Encyclopedia of American History*. New York: Harper & Row, 1965.

Nash, Gary B. *Red, White, and Black*. Englewood Cliffs, NJ: Prentice-Hall, 1974.

Nell, William C. *Colored Patriots of the American Revolution*. Salem, NH: Ayer, 1986.

Patrick, Denise Lewis. *Jackie Robinson: Strong Inside and Out*. New York: HarperCollins, 2005.

Ploski, Harry A., and James Williams. *The Negro Almanac.* New York: Gale Research, 1989.

Preszler, June. *Juneteenth: Jubilee for Freedom.* Mankato, MN: Capstone Press, 2007.

Quarles, Benjamin. *Black Abolitionists.* New York: Da Capo Press, 1969.

Quarles, Benjamin. *The Negro in the American Revolution.* New York: W. W. Norton, 1961.

Quarles, Benjamin. *The Negro in the Civil War.* Boston: Little, Brown & Company, 1969.

Robinson, Jackie, and Alfred Duckett. *Breakthrough to the Big League.* Lakeville, CT: Grey Castle Press, 1965.

Sertima, Ivan Van. *They Came Before Columbus.* New York: Random House, 1976.

Sherman, Joan R., Ed. *The Black Bard of North Carolina: George Moses Horton and His Poetry.* Chapel Hill: The University of North Carolina Press, 1997.

Smith, Jessie Carney. *Black Firsts.* Detroit: Visible Ink Press, 1994.

Smith, Jessie Carney. *Notable Black American Men.* Detroit: Gale Group, 1999.

Smith, Sande. *Who's Who in African American History.* New York: Smithmark, 1994.

Stewart, Jeffrey C. *1001 Things Everyone Should Know about African American History.* New York: Main Street Books, 1996.

Still, William. *The Underground Railroad.* Philadelphia: Porter and Coates, 1872. Accessed on www.gutenberg.org.

Taylor, Charles A. *Juneteenth: A Celebration of Freedom.* Greensboro, NC: Open Hand, 2002.

Weber, Michael. *The American Revolution.* New York: Raintree Steck-Vaughn, 2000.

Wesley, Charles H. *International Library of Afro-American Life and History: In Freedom's Footsteps.* Cornwells Heights, PA: The Publishers Agency, 1978.

Wesley, Charles H. *International Library of Afro-American Life and History: The Quest for Equality.* Cornwells Heights, PA: The Publishers Agency, 1978.

Wesley, Charles H., and Patricia W. Romero. *International Library of Afro-American Life and History: Afro-Americans in the Civil War.* Cornwells Heights, PA: The Publishers Agency, 1978.

Wexler, Sanford. *The Civil Rights Movement.* New York: Facts on File, 1999.

Whitlow, Roger. *Black American Literature.* Chicago: Nelson Hall, 1973.

Williams, Michael W., Ed. *The African American Encyclopedia.* Volumes 1–8. New York: Marshall Cavendish, 1993.

Winch, Julie. *A Gentleman of Color: The Life of James Forten.* New York: Oxford University Press, 2002.

Wright, Kai. *Soldiers of Freedom.* New York: Black Dog and Leventhal, 2002.

Letters

William Lloyd Garrison to Robert Purvis, June 22, 1832, Boston Public Library.

William Lloyd Garrison to Robert Purvis, December 10, 1832, Boston Public Library.

Web Site Sources

http://americanabolitionist.liberalarts.iupui.edu/nell.htm

http://bioguide.congress.gov

http://blackhistorypages.net

http://brainstorm-services.com/wcu/langston-hughes.html

http://celebrateboston.com/sites/salem.htm

http://dbs.ohiohistory.org/africanam/page.cfm?ID=5557

http://digital.library.okstate.edu/encyclopedia/entries/R/RE020.html

http://docsouth.unc.edu/

http://edison.rutgers.edu/latimer/blueprnt.htm

http://encyclopediaofarkansas.net

http://en.wikipedia.org

http://esperstamps.org/aa6.htm

http://history-is-made-at-night.blogspot.com/2007/01/rent-parties.html

http://home.wlu.edu

http://mac110.assumption.edu/aas/Intros/soldiers.html

http://memory.loc.gov

http://mistupid.com/sports/worldseries.htm

http://mlb.mlb.com

http://news.bbc.co.uk/2/hi/africa/1068950.stm

http://nmaahc.si.edu/

http://northbysouth.kenyon.edu/1998/pages/savage.htm

www.aaregistry.com

www.acmewebpages.com/dodgers/1955team.htm

www.africanamericans.com

www.allmediaproductions.com/mali.html

www.americanhistory.si.edu

www.americaslibrary.gov

www.arlingtoncemetery.net

www.artcyclopedia.com/artists/savage_augusta.html

www.baseball-almanac.com/ws/yr1955ws.shtml

www.baseball-reference.com

www.cem.va.gov/pdf/beaufort.pdf

www.civilwarconsortium.org/juneteenth/about.html

www.cwo.com/~lucumi/race.html

www.dalnet.lib.mi.us

www.digitalhistory.uh.edu

www.dpw-archives.org

www.explorepahistory.com

www.fairhillburial.org

www.gwu.edu/~e73afram/abm-kf-am.html

www.geocities.com/Hayesportfolio/rent_parties.htm

www.geocities.com/Heartland/Pointe/6765/purvisfam.html

www.geocities.com/SoHo/Workshop/4275/StJohnsLec1

www.historycooperative.org

www.history.rochester.edu/class/douglass/

www.historyswomen.com/admire/Admire20.html

www.iupui.edu/~douglass/documents_letters.htm#1847

www.juneteenth.com

www.learningtogive.org/lessons/attach_num=1&ln=5&unit=133

www.legendsofamerica.com

www.libraries.wvu.edu/delany/masint.htm

www.library.upenn.edu/collections/rbm/photos/anderson/3967.html

www.literarytraveler.com/authors/zora_neale_hurston.aspx

www.loc.gov

www.mariananderson.org

www.math.buffalo.edu/~sww/0history/hwny-douglass-family.html

www.nasm.si.edu/blackwings/hstudent/bio_anderson.cfm

www.nationalcowboymuseum.org

www.nccusa.org

www.nps.gov

www.nr.org

www.nsbcdc.org

www.nwhm.org/RightsforWomen/Burroughs.html

www.nypl.org

www.octobergallery.com/artists/burke.htm

www.pbs.org/wgbh/aia/home.html

www.pmphoto.to/WorldsFairTour/Zone-2/the-harp.htm

www.poets.org/viewmedia.php/prmMID/15722

www.press.uchicago.edu/Misc/Chicago/333302.html

www.primaryresearch.org

www.routledge-ny.com/ref/harlem/parties.html

www.stanford.edu/group/King/publications/papers/vol4/580308-003-To_Nannie_Helen_
    Burroughs.htm

www.streetswing.com/histmain/d5rent1.htm

www.suite101.com/article.cfm/biographies_scientists/83592

www.tcjn.edu/~messmer2/rent_parties.html

www.texancultures.utsa.edu/publications/exploration/chapternine.htm

www.texasmilitaryforcesmuseum.org/wortham/4345.htm

www.thecrisismagazine.com

www.thehistorymakers.com

www.theoutlaws.com/lawmen2.htm

www.tsha.utexas.edu

www.tsl.state.tx.us/ref/abouttx/juneteenth.html

www.tuskegee.edu

www.uafortsmith.edu/News/Index?storyid=1659

www.washingtonpost.com/wp-dyn/articles/A52868-2004Aug9.html

www.whenweruled.com/articles.php?Ing=en&pg=5

www.whitehouse.gov

About the Authors

Jeff has taught at Fairmont Elementary School in Yorba Linda, California, for most of his 25-year career as an elementary classroom teacher. Recently winning the prestigious 2007 Blue Ribbon Award as well as the 2006 Distinguished School Award, Fairmont Elementary School has been like a second home to Jeff. He truly feels connected to the staff as well as past, present, and future students and their parents as part of his extended family.

This is Jeff and Nancy's third book together. After they wrote their first, *15 Fun-to-Read American History Mini-Books* (2000), they enjoyed the collaborative process so much that they decided to continue on as a writing team.

Nancy is the best-selling author of more than seventy books. Her newest picture book, *D Is for Drinking Gourd: An African American Alphabet* (2007), is a winner of the 2007 NAPPA Honors book award and was selected for the 2008 IRA Teachers' Choice List. It was also chosen for the Notable Social Studies Trade Books for Young People 2008. Caldecott Honor award–winning illustrator E. B. Lewis illustrated the book.

Nancy specializes in writing about African American history for kids. She loves to explore local university bookshelves and discover primary sources along with amazing information and little-known or nearly forgotten facts about the history of African Americans. Jeff is a valuable contributor to the research process and also keeps Nancy posted on current events so they can share precious nuggets of important knowledge with children through books.

Together in the spring of 2007, Jeff and Nancy toured historic places from the founding years of our nation, such as the African Burial Grounds in New York City, the site of James Forten's home in Philadelphia, and Sally Heming's residence at Monticello. On Juneteenth, they visited the historic Richard Allen Museum in the lower level of the beautiful Mother Bethel A.M.E. Church in Philadelphia.

Nancy has written numerous books for teachers with Scholastic's Teaching Resources including the best-seller *25 Read and Write Mini-Books that Teach Word Families* and its two series companions: *25 Read and Write Mini-Books that Teach Phonics* and *26 Read and Write Mini-Books that Teach Beginning Sounds*. She has also written various readers script plays for the early elementary classroom including *15 Easy-to-Read Nursery Rhyme Mini-Book Plays*. She is currently working on several books to feature our nation's African American founding fathers and mothers. Her Web site can be found at www.nancyisanders.com and her blog at www.nancyisanders.wordpress.com. Both are places where teachers may find a selection of classroom resources as well as opportunities for students to take a behind-the-scenes glimpse at the life of a published author.